D0431686

me,
you
&
the
kids,
too

me, you & the kids, too

Renée Elliott

DUNCAN BAIRD PUBLISHERS

LONDON

ME, YOU & THE KIDS, TOO
Renée Elliott

Distributed in the USA and Canada by
Sterling Publishing Co., Inc.
387 Park Avenue South
New York, NY 10016-8810

First published in the UK and USA in 2012 by
Duncan Baird Publishers Ltd
Sixth Floor, Castle House, 75–76 Wells Street
London W1T 3QH

Managing Editor: Grace Cheetham
Editors: Nicole Bator, Gillian Haslam and Krissy Mallett
Managing Designer: Manisha Patel
Designer: Blok Graphic
Production: Uzma Taj
Commissioned Photography: Dan Jones
Artwork: Jessica Elliott and Nicholas Elliott
Food Stylists: Bianca Nice and Sue Henderson
Prop Stylist: Sue Rowlands

Library of Congress Cataloging-in-Publication Data available

ISBN: 978-1-84899-012-8

10 9 8 7 6 5 4 3 2 1

Typeset in Scala Sans and ITC American Typewriter
Color reproduction by Colourscan
Printed in Singapore by Imago

For information about custom editions, special sales, premium
and corporate purchases, please contact Sterling Special Sales
Department at 800-805-5489 or specialsales@sterlingpub.com.

*To my mom, Lucille, and my dad, Edward. And also
to Grace, my editor, who gave this book so much.*

Vegetarian Recipes
Vegetarian recipes in this book contain no meat, poultry,
game, fish or shellfish. They may include eggs or cheese.
Cheese, especially those made using traditional methods,
may contain calf rennet, so check labels first. Look for
"suitable for vegetarians", the "V" sign or "contains
vegetarian rennet" on the label.

Unless otherwise stated:
• All recipes serve 2 adults, 1 child and 1 baby
• Preparation and cooking times refer to only the
  main recipes
• Use organic ingredients
• Use wild salmon
• Use extra-large eggs
• Use medium fruit and vegetables
• Use fresh ingredients, including herbs
• 1 tsp. = 5ml 1 tbsp. = 15ml 1 cup = 240ml

Acknowledgments
The biggest thanks must go to my husband Brian. He is
my rock. He ate all of the food and took care of the children.
Thanks to my kids Jess, Nicholas and Cassie, who wanted
me to be with them all of the time, but let me work. And
thanks to Jess and Nicholas, who were part of the
photography and drew the pictures that are in the book.

There would not be a book—or it would not be so
perfect—without Grace, Krissy, Nicole, Gillian, Manisha
and Allan. A huge thank you to Borra for always listening,
and for her support and encouragement.

And a sweet thank you to Niamh, Zoë and Josie who
were also photographed.

I wanted this book to be triple tested—and not just by
me. There is a huge and heartfelt thank you for the recipe
testers who cooked and baked for me—my mother, Lucille,
my brother, David, and my sisters, Jan and Lauren. And
thank you to my friends, Allison, Annabel, Jazz, Julia, Julie,
Kate and Simon. They cooked my creations for themselves,
their children, their builders—and their friends. And
everyone came back with ideas and suggestions and
comments that helped shape this book into something
much better than it was. Like any journey, it's better
traveled in the company of family and friends.

Contents

Introduction

A friend once said to me that raising kids is simple—all you have to do is marinate them in love for 18 years and then send them out into the world. I agree with this completely and from my perspective, the second priority—if you want them to be strong, live well and fulfill their potential—is to feed them nutritious food so that they have good health. Without well-being, it is difficult or impossible to do anything. Yet with a foundation of health and vitality, your children can pursue their dreams.

Before I had my eldest daughter, Jessica, I was a pretty good cook. I had been working in natural foods for ten years and cared about what I ate. I made home-cooked food and liked to bake occasionally. When Jessie was born, I happily breast-fed her for four months, but when she started to reach for my spoon, I realized that I actually had no idea how or what to cook for a baby. I hadn't planned on giving her jarred baby food because I knew instinctively that I wanted

to give her fresh, homemade meals. But, other than that, I didn't know what to do.

I knew I didn't want her to have refined foods, like white rice and white flour, because they are so low in nutrition, and I wondered whether she should be eating things like gluten, dairy or soya early on. I found one great book, did lots of nutritional research and quizzed many experts—and formulated a feeding plan as I went. I took notes on recipes I created and techniques I discovered and carried on in the same way when I had my second child, Nicholas. My babies flourished and when my youngest, Cassandra, was ready to wean, I wrote it all down in my first book, *Healthy Eating for Your Baby & Toddler*.

However, with work and three young children, I was so tired and busy, that cooking for myself and my husband, Brian, was too often an afterthought. I knew that I had to be well nourished in order to be able to take care of everyone else, but I would make gorgeous meals for them and then wonder what on earth we were going to eat. And I was often too befuddled from the broken nights to figure it out.

My editor, Grace, who had a young baby, was going through the same experience. She said, "What we need is a book for the whole family—a book that helps people cook great meals for themselves, as well as their kids, so they can take care of their needs at the same time as providing the best start for their baby." And so this book was born.

This book is filled with the most nourishing and delicious meals for you and your family. Just pick a recipe and, from that recipe, comes food for you, your partner and your kids—as well as a step-by-step guide to preparing a meal for your baby at the same time. You don't need extra ingredients and it's all worked out for you—whether you have a 6 to 9 or 9 to 12 month old.

Like all parents, I don't always do a perfect job. But I have managed to incorporate some solid nutritional basics into our daily and weekly routines, such as using wholewheat flours, eating different grains and

including superfoods such as seaweeds and seeds.

You'll never begin all of them at once, so just take it slowly. However, I hope that you will be inspired to pick some things out of the book that spark your interest and gradually try to make each one a habit—like changing your baking to use wholegrain spelt flour or not purchasing sweetened breakfast cereals.

When you decide you want a baby and imagine lying on the couch snuggling your little one, the last thing on your mind is the amount of cooking you will be doing for that little person. But even if cooking isn't really your thing—or hasn't been up until now—it's a fact of life that if you want to make nourishing food, then someone needs to get in the kitchen!

There is a lot of food to prepare for kids who can't do anything for themselves in the kitchen for many years. I realized that I needed to work out a way to make my family's meals easily—without having to take time from all of the other things I needed to do (like working and getting some sleep myself).

However, this book isn't just about cooking for your baby and kids; it's about cooking great meals for you and your partner, too. You'll find it easy to cook something delicious for yourselves and enjoy some time together in the evening, all the while making sure you're nourishing yourself.

Although some of these recipes may take time on the hob or in the oven, they are all very simple to make —using quick preparation techniques and very easy steps to follow. And while you're cooking the meal, you can blend up a meal for your baby, too. You don't have to work anything out, and the recipes make cooking for your baby a breeze because you're using the same ingredients for your meal.

How this book works

This book is for feeding the whole family and, unless otherwise stated, the recipes are for two adults, one young child and one baby. You can choose a recipe and cook it for you and your family. Simply make a little more of the recipe if you're feeding more than one child and if you're cooking for just you and your partner, you'll have leftovers for the following day, or for your freezer. If you want to cook for a 6 to 9 month old or a 9 to 12 month old, simply make it when you make the main meal.

As you follow the method for the main recipe, you will see signs showing (6-9) or (9-12)—these tell you when you need to set aside some of the ingredients or mixture for your baby. Then go to the corresponding method for either age group and follow that method to make the extra meal. Because the types of foods that your baby can eat increase at every stage of development, the recipes for the 9 to 12 month old build on the recipes for the 6 to 9 month old. When your baby is a year old, you can use the main recipe.

For 6 to 9 months, you need a good selection of purees made from the foods listed in the chart on page 20. From 9 to 12 months, you can include more foods and you can either make a lumpy puree or try some small pieces of food. From 12 months onward, your child can eat what you eat—although you may want to go easy on spices and strong flavors, and continue to avoid salt.

I have made all the recipes as simple as possible. When I read recipes that want me to steam or sauté vegetables beforehand or have lots of separate fiddly steps, I assume they are not aimed at someone with a baby. When you are a parent, you need things to be really simple and easy because you have so much else going on. So, for example, before I make the quiche, I don't steam the broccoli as it will cook in the oven, and I don't sauté the onions. The flavors are still great —and the whole recipe is incredibly quick to make.

Don't be put off trying a recipe that has an ingredient you are not familiar with. In the ingredients list, it may say yogurt or kefir, wholegrain spelt flour or

wholewheat flour, so buy what is easier for you. After you have tried a recipe, like it and want to make it again, then try the more unusual ingredient. My goal is to introduce you gradually to different and better foods and expand your palate and repertoire of ingredients.

Also, don't worry about buying unusual ingredients such as kuzu and quinoa, that you think you won't use up. There are enough recipes in the book to use these great ingredients. Don't be afraid to buy something that you've never used before or don't know if you will like. If you make one dish that isn't your favorite, the index can help you find other recipes using specific ingredients.

I love making my own beans but you may not have the time, so buy canned ones instead. Don't worry—it's something you can choose to do in the future. What I'm saying is don't *not* try a recipe because of that. You've got to make your life easy. I am showing you the most nutritious way to prepare food, but it has to work in your life at the time.

Why healthy?

Without doubt, what your baby eats affects his or her health today and in the future. If your child starts off eating a narrow range of foods, he or she will probably continue doing so throughout his or her life—and may not get a complete spectrum of nutrients. This can impact on his or her health both in the formative years and also later in life.

Eating a wide range of foods creates a strong foundation of health and increases your chance of getting the necessary nutrients. It creates adventurous eating in your children as they grow, and if they ever get finicky about what they eat, they will still have a wide range of foods to choose from. You can get children used to healthy tastes from an early age and this will nourish them for rest of their lives. Even if your child rebels against your cooking and wholewheat bread at some point, the likelihood is that he or she will come back to what he or she knows—and the tastes that are familiar … eventually.

So think about shaping your children's palates to love foods such as unsweetened yogurt, unsweetened oatmeal, wholewheat pasta, sourdough rye, sprouts, nuts and seeds. And because treats like chocolate are probably inevitable, and so delectable, you don't have to forbid them—but choose the best, which is semi-sweet, organic chocolate.

Why organic?
There's a question. Yes, yes, there are so many labels out there. How could you possibly choose? Well, it's really quite simple. If you want the best-quality food, choose organic. If you want meat and dairy products that don't carry antibiotic residues; if you want fruit and vegetables without pesticide residues; if you want to eat food that is free from genetically modified ingredients; and if you don't want to have to examine food labels to ensure the food doesn't contain any nasty additives, choose organic.

If you find it difficult to find everything organically or if it's too expensive, start with what you eat the most of, and also opt for organic fruit and vegetables. If you can buy organic dairy products, which are higher in essential fatty acids and other essential nutrients, that's an added bonus. Organic meat is expensive to farm and therefore costs more. So rather than spend more on meat, you can buy less of it and eat better quality.

What is healthy food?
Healthy food is everything that nature hands directly to us—seeds, nuts, beans, vegetables, fruits, grains, fish and meat. When you cook at home using these ingredients, the meals you make will nourish and sustain you.

The most basic advice for healthy eating is this: avoid highly-processed foods, candies, fried foods, junk food, soft drinks, white flour, sugar, salt and cheap fats. Instead, fill yourselves with natural ingredients that are full of nutrients. If you can eat a rainbow of foods every day—a whole range of different-colored foods—you'll be doing well. And if you can add superfoods in, too, you'll be doing brilliantly. Try the recipes—and try the superfood ingredients, even if you've never heard of them and have to order them from a health food store. I've worked out easy ways to incorporate them into your recipes—and into your life.

Healthy food for the whole family

What do I feed my baby?

When a baby is born, he or she is ready only for mother's milk. At any time after 4 months, a baby may want solid foods. There is much debate about how long you should breast feed and at what age you should introduce solids, but I think if you pay attention to your child and listen to your intuition, you will know when the time is right. My first daughter, Jessica, who was very little when she was born, couldn't take her eyes off my fork when she was 4 months old so I weaned her then. Whatever you do, the most important thing is to start very, very gently.

For the first two years, a baby's digestive and immune systems are not fully developed. For this reason, it is sensible to introduce foods carefully. That is why I wait to introduce certain foods until they have developed a little more. For example, I don't introduce dairy (other than yogurt for soaking) until 9 to 12 months and I leave introducing gluten, foods in the deadly nightshade family (tomatoes, eggplants, potatoes and so on) and yeasty foods such as mushrooms until 1 year. Many of these foods are either harder to digest or are associated with allergies. We may not know for a very long time—if ever—what the perfect foods are for a baby to eat at each stage,

but this approach is thoughtful and mindful of the limitations of an immature and developing body. If you want to avoid cow milk, your baby can get great calcium at different stages from yogurt, cheese, dark green vegetables (broccoli, kale, spinach, turnip greens and collard greens), oranges, tempeh, peas, black beans, sardines, sesame seeds and almonds.

Meals for everyone

It's important that each day everyone in the family has a good balance of protein, carbohydrates, vegetables and fat. There is protein in meats, fish, dairy products, eggs, beans, whole grains, vegetables, nuts and seeds. This book provides healthy meals for everyone—from parents or carers to toddlers and the baby who's just starting to enjoy food. Good health comes from the ingredients, the wholeness and the way you cook them —for example, if you soak and steam. If you eat like this some or most of the time, you'll be doing really well.

All you hear about these days is to avoid sugar, salt and fat. Well, it's more complicated than that and I don't think you can say "don't do this" and then not talk about the better alternatives. That's what this section is about. And it's about moderation.

Sugar

I'm not crazy about sugar. I love the taste of it, but I hate what it does to the body, especially over a long period of time. It creates stress by forcing your body to adjust to the high blood sugar levels it creates. If this stress continues over a long period, it can lead to type 2 diabetes. Furthermore, too much sugar in your body gets converted to fat.

I see two huge problems around sugar. One is having desserts every day or after every meal, which can lead to a terrible lifelong habit. And the other is that sugar isn't just found in sweet things—it's also in many savory processed foods, too. Reduce the sugar that you eat, cut down on desserts and avoid giving it to your baby for as long as you possibly can.

Organic cane sugar is better than conventional white refined sugar because of the processing involved, but rice malt syrup and agave stand head and shoulders above all sweeteners. Rice malt syrup, a delicately flavored natural sweetener, is made up mostly of complex sugars and, therefore, unlike white sugar, releases slowly into the bloodstream.

Salt

There is bad salt and there is good salt. Much salt is so over-refined that manufacturers add iodine back into it. Babies don't need it, but as children grow up, it's not the salt in your cooking that will be a problem, but the salt in snacks, such as potato chips, junk food and processed meals, which are cheaply made and rely on salt for flavor. Use a good sea salt moderately in your cooking. I have specified amounts of salt in each recipe to give you guidelines on healthy quantities.

Fats

Fats are necessary and important in our diets. They provide energy, they are building blocks for cell membranes and hormones, they keep us full, carry fat-soluble vitamins and support many other body processes. However, there is good fat and bad fat. Play it smart. Don't buy anything that contains hydrogenated or partially hydrogenated fat and reduce or eliminate the amount of fried foods you eat.

But do enjoy cold-pressed seed oils to get the essential good fats that your body needs every day. Don't worry about eating fat in dairy products and in good-quality meats. It's the fat that gives it the flavor (you often find low-fat yogurts have a lot of added sugar to give them flavor) and babies need good fat. Buy butter, not margarine, and whole yogurt—and cut out cheap and greasy snack foods.

Milk

I firmly believe that cow milk is meant for baby cows, not for human beings. Our digestive systems are not designed to process cow milk and it can cause real health problems in many children and adults. You'll find that there are wonderful alternatives available— you can use rice milk, oat milk or water instead of milk. All the recipes in this book suggest these alternatives.

Meat

What's important is to eat good-quality, grass-fed meats. It makes sense to spend the same amount of money per week on meat, but buy organic, which is more expensive to produce but much better quality. In the food pyramid, remember that as well as meat, protein is found in poultry, fish, beans, eggs, nuts and seeds. Stay away from sausages, luncheon meats and other processed meats, which aren't worth eating.

Whole grains

Whole grains are full of goodness. As well as vitamins and minerals, they also contain valuable protein. What's more, you can enhance their nutritional status. When our ancestors ate whole grains, they didn't eat quick-rise breads and hastily prepared oatmeal. They soaked or fermented grains first. And, of course, there is a good reason for this.

Soaking whole grains allows two important processes to take place. All grains contain phytic acid in the outer layer. In our bodies, the phytic acid binds with calcium, copper, iron, magnesium and zinc (for a strong immune system) and prevents us from absorbing them. Neutralizing the phytic acid is done simply by soaking the grain in warm acidulated water at least seven hours. Soaking with a spoonful of yogurt lets enzymes, such as lactobacilli, break down and neutralize the phytic acid. The other beneficial reason is that soaking grains in warm water encourages them to produce their own enzymes, which then increases the quantity of B vitamins you will eat.

When a recipe says serve with rice or a grain, try the following variations:

RICE: black, brown basmati, jasmine, long-grain, red Camargue, short-grain and wild.
GRAINS: amaranth, barley, buckwheat, corn, Kamut, millet, oat, quinoa, rye, spelt and wheat.
FLAKES: barley, buckwheat, Kamut, millet, oat, quinoa, rice, rye, spelt and wheat.
FLOURS: barley, buckwheat, chestnut, chickpea, coconut, corn, Kamut, oat, rye, spelt and wheat.

Wholewheat flour

Nature has given us all of the goodness and fiber we need in a grain if we eat the whole thing, which is why you should eat wholewheat flour whenever possible.

There isn't a lot of point in eating white flour as manufacturers remove the two most nutritious and fiber-rich parts of the seed—the outside bran layer and the inside germ. It is so stripped of its goodness that synthetic vitamins are added back into it. To add insult to injury, white flour is then bleached. Your body can't tell the difference between white sugar and white flour.

White flour is the other sugar.

When someone eats refined carbohydrates (white flour, cereals, bread, biscuits, snacks) or simple sugars, they require very little metabolism by the body, so they enter the bloodstream rapidly. This causes a quick rise in blood sugar levels, which triggers a similarly rapid release of the body's sugar-regulating hormone, insulin. This gives you the 'lift' followed by the 'crash', which makes you feel tired and down. If this happens over a long period of time, it may lead to thrombosis, high blood pressure, heart disease, hypoglycemia, type 2 diabetes, decreased immune function and adrenal stress. Try not to cook white rice or pasta at home. You can eat it sometimes, but have it when out at restaurants or friends' houses and eat the good stuff at home.

Adding nutrition

As food plays such a huge part in our health, I like to add extra nutrition wherever possible (this is especially important with children who may not be big eaters). That's why I like to use ingredients like kuzu and miso (see pages 15 and 16) instead of cornstarch and salt. Also try serving a little nori at mealtime, sprinkling furikake (a mix of sesame seeds and seaweed) on your child's rice or pasta and adding sprouts in when you can. And give them healthy snacks between meals, such as tahini on rice crackers, fruit, vegetable sticks, unsweetened popcorn, nuts and seeds.

Helpful hints

If you want to make changes to the way you eat, don't try to do everything at once. If you do, the chances are that it won't be fun or enjoyable, you will become stressed and you'll go back to the way you were eating before. Try changing one thing a month or every few months. Make it simple, like switching to wholewheat bread or buying unsweetened organic yogurt. Eat some raw and cooked vegetables, of different colours, at every meal. Eat a rainbow of foods every day. Get your kids cooking with you as soon as they are interested. If you have older children, look at their favorite foods and make subtle, healthy changes. For example, if they love pizza, make it with wholewheat crust. If they eat salad, add seeds. Mix plain yogurt into homemade cereal, instead of highly-processed breakfast cereals.

Wonderfoods

Other than apple, avocado and broccoli, I'm not going to talk about most of the usual wonder- or superfoods. All fresh, organic foods as basic ingredients are quite wonderful and have something special about the nutrients they offer us. They are more wonderful when you eat them in season, because they are at their optimum in terms of growing and ripening. Most of the foods listed below are special because they offer something above and beyond what most people eat every day and are worth including in your diet.

Amaranth

Originally found in South America and Mexico, amaranth dates back about 8,000 years in the human diet. It is packed with nutrients and is 15 to 17 percent protein. Amaranth is vitamin rich and a good source of vitamins A, B6, C, folate and riboflavin. It has lots of minerals and is loaded with fiber. Amaranth benefits the immune system, helps with hypertension and cardiovascular disease. And it tastes good.

Apple

You've got to love apples! They are always available, easy to grow and store, inexpensive and truly and simply delicious. Not only that, but they also increase bone density, reduce wheezing from asthma, protect against lung, breast, colon and liver cancers and Alzheimer's, help with diabetes and can help you lose weight.

Avocado

Ah, one of my four favorite foods. Avocado is considered by many to be a perfect food because it is so good for you. It is absolutely wonderful for babies, providing them with fabulous fat and filling them up with goodness. Avocado is the best fruit source of vitamin E, which is great for overall health. It is also good for your eyes, heart, skin, prostate, absorption of food nutrients, and helps to prevent different cancers of the mouth, skin and prostate because of its special mix of anti-inflammatory and antioxidant nutrients.

Cut in half, remove the stone and fill the hole with oil and vinegar. Add slices to sandwiches—especially good with hummus—or salads. Mash it into a dip or guacamole or blend it into a smoothie.

Broccoli

Broccoli is part of the cruciferous family of vegetables, which are so good for you that they should be eaten at least three times a week. Steaming is the best way to eat broccoli because it retains its goodness, stays slightly crunchy and most kids really love it cooked

that way. Don't overcook it to the point where it is dark and mushy. Broccoli helps metabolize vitamin D, it helps the body detoxify and it lessens the effect of allergens in our bodies.

Buckwheat

Another great grain to add into your diet, buckwheat has a wonderful nutritional profile. One of its benefits is that it contains almost 86 milligrams of magnesium in 1 cup. Magnesium relaxes blood vessels, improves blood flow and, therefore, the delivery of nutrients throughout the body while reducing blood pressure. A complex carbohydrate, buckwheat is energizing whether you have it as a hot cereal for breakfast or as part of your lunch or dinner.

Garlic

Garlic has two main beneficial effects on the body. The first is that it is a powerful and natural antibiotic and antifungal, and the second is that it is good for the immune system.

I used to think of garlic as a cooking condiment, but now I use it as a vegetable in its own right. I used to consider that three cloves of garlic was a lot, but now I always seem to use an entire head.

Kefir

Kefir is called a miracle food. It is made by culturing fresh milk, water and kefir grains, which are clumps of bacteria proven to be highly beneficial to our digestive system. Kefir is similar to yogurt in taste, but as well as containing healthy bacteria, kefir also contains healthy yeasts. Kefir enhances the microorganisms of the intestines, which assist in digestion. It stimulates the immune system, protects against harmful bacteria and is packed with vitamins, minerals, amino acids and enzymes.

Kuzu

You probably use a thickening agent in some of your cooking, but instead of using cornstarch, which has no nutritional value and is heavily bleached (unless organic), you could switch to kuzu, a starch made from the root of the kuzu or kudzu plant. Plants concentrate their energy in their roots, which is why root vegetables are so valuable to eat and why some roots, such as

ginseng, are known for their medicinal qualities.

In Japan and China, kuzu is known for its excellence as a thickening and jelling agent and for its healing properties for digestive disorders, such as stomach aches and diarrhea. Kuzu is full of flavonoids, which relax constricted blood vessels. This means it can help ease headaches, migraines and high blood pressure. Kuzu also neutralizes lactic acid and eliminates it from the body, and relaxes tight muscles.

Kuzu comes in chunks. Crush it into a powder with the back of a spoon and use about 1½ tablespoons of kuzu to each 1 cup of liquid for sauces and gravies, and 2 tablespoons per 1 cup of liquid for jelling.

Millet

A great and underused gluten-free grain, millet is highly nutritious and alkaline, easy to digest and soothing to the digestive system. It is called by some the most digestible and least allergenic grain in the world. Nearly 15 percent protein, millet is also high in fiber, the B vitamins, vitamin E and important minerals. Great for a hot cereal in the morning or instead of pasta or rice.

Miso

A fermented soya product, miso is delicious, useful and medicinal. You can use miso instead of salt in soups and casseroles to add a richness of flavor. Miso is a good source of amino acids and is like yogurt in that it is full of lactic-acid bacteria and enzymes that aid digestion. Recent scientific research shows that miso helps the body get rid of some carcinogens, acidity, radiation and the effects of smoking and pollution.

At the end of cooking, take some of the broth from the soup or stew, dissolve a tablespoon or so of miso in it, then stir it back in. It may be briefly simmered, but boiling miso will destroy its health-giving properties.

Nuts

Nuts are one of the best plant sources of protein. They are high in good fats and rich in fiber, phytonutrients and antioxidants. Almonds are particularly fabulous and I always have a bowl of them out for the kids to snack on. Almonds help to regulate blood pressure, prevent cancer, protect against diabetes, boost your energy, reduce risk of heart disease, improve brain power and prevent birth defects. Peanuts, however, should wait until your child is 5 years old.

Oils

Your body needs essential fatty acids every day because it can't manufacture them from other things you eat. Cold-pressed seed oils are an excellent source of essential fats. Choose from flax, hemp, pumpkin, safflower, sesame and sunflower. Hemp is the best oil, but any of these will do your baby a world of good. These oils are so important, that you should aim to add a teaspoon of cold-pressed seed oil to one meal each day for your baby—and for you. You can start with his or her first foods, with 1 teaspoon a day from 4 months old, increasing to 2 teaspoons from 6 months.

Always choose extra virgin olive oil as it is the juice extracted from the first pressing of olives (unlike virgin olive oil, which is made by mixing and refining much lower grade oil). Extra virgin olive oil is wonderful for us because of its high monounsaturated fat content in the form of oleic acid (between 60 and 80 percent), which studies have shown to reduce LDL cholesterol levels. Research has also linked oleic acid to a

reduction in the growth of many types of cancer cells. Up to 20 percent of extra virgin olive oil is also made up of essential omega-6 fatty acids. Added to this, the polyphenol antioxidants and vitamin E present in extra virgin olive oil make it a very healthy fat indeed.

Quinoa

Quinoa (pronounced keen-wah) is an ancient grain from South America. It is rich in protein, including all nine amino acids, and especially rich in lysine. Lysine is needed by the body for growth and repair so it is vital for growing children and all of us as we get older.

Quinoa is a good source of manganese, magnesium, iron, copper and phosphorus, which means it is important for people who have migraines, diabetes and atherosclerosis. When cooked, quinoa has a fluffy, creamy texture and a slight nutty flavor, and works well as a replacement for rice and couscous.

Sardines

Sardines really are the best fish you can eat. Not only are so many fish these days being overfished, but many of them also contain dangerous levels of toxins because we pollute our oceans so badly. Farmed fish are not an option because they are raised in poor conditions, like intensively-farmed animals (with organic as the only exception). Sardines are so low down on the food chain that they don't carry toxins like other fish, especially large fish such as tuna.

Sardines are good for cardiovascular health, memory, joints, energy and skin. In addition, they are also a stunning source of omega-3 essential fats. If you start your baby on sardines young, he or she will love them. If you are not so keen on them, try the fishcakes on page 59. If you and your kids like sardines, try to slot them into your weekly routine. They are a great fast food and make an easy lunch served on toast with mayonnaise or on crispbreads.

Seaweeds

Dried seaweeds probably contain more minerals than any other kind of food. They are rich in essential minerals, vitamins, protein and important trace minerals—many of which are no longer in our exhausted soil. They contain all of the elements essential to health, including calcium, sodium, magnesium, potassium, iodine, iron and zinc. Seaweeds also contain important vitamins, including trace amounts of B12, which rarely occur in land vegetables.

If you've never used seaweed and don't understand it, now is a great time to add it to your ingredient list. I would suggest you start with two or three different kinds, such as kombu, nori and arame. If you buy these for your pantry, you will soon finish them off as you try the recipes in this book.

If you want to cook your own beans, buy dried and cook them with kombu. Your kids will love nori straight from the package or you can mix it with salads, pastas or rice dishes. Either buy sushi nori that is already toasted or buy plain and toast it quickly over a gas flame until it turns green. Arame can be used with zucchini (see page 126) or can be crumbled, soaked and mixed into pasta or rice dishes without adding too strong a flavor.

Seeds

Seeds are nature's little powerhouses. They are loaded with protein and oil. Try adding them to yogurt, oatmeal or cereals for breakfast. Toss them into salads, pasta and rice dishes for lunch or dinner. And put little bowls of them out to encourage your children—and you—to snack on them during the day. You get their full benefit when you eat them raw, but toasting them lightly—or with tamari, if you wish—makes them pretty irresistible. If possible, store seeds in the refrigerator to keep them fresh so you receive the full benefit of their oils.

Sprouts

Packed with goodness, sprouts such as alfalfa, broccoli and mung contain an abundance of highly active antioxidants that prevent DNA destruction and protect us from the ongoing effects of ageing. They are also valued because they help to protect us from disease, increase bone formation and prevent bone breakdown, help control tumors and hot flashes, support the immune system—the list goes on and on.

Great tasting, sprouts can be used in many ways —use them to liven up a plain sandwich, add them to salads, use them in wraps, mix them with rice and include them in sushi. My daughter, Jessie, eats them

as a little salad on their own, tossed with olive oil and a little balsamic vinegar. If you have a good health food store near you, you can find sprouts such as aduki, fenugreek, chickpea, lentil, mung, radish, sunflower and more. If not, they are easy to grow at home if you buy a sprouting kit.

Yogurt

The biggest reason to eat yogurt on a regular basis is for the good gut bacteria it contains. Forget those little yogurt drinks that are loaded with sugar. Eat plain whole yogurt as it has so much flavor and creaminess that you don't need sugar. Yogurt is an excellent source of protein, calcium, vitamin D, riboflavin and vitamins B6 and B12—and much better to eat than milk because it has gone through a fermentation process that breaks down the milk sugar (lactose) and the milk protein (casein) for us. It also restores many of the enzymes, which are destroyed when milk is pasteurized, that help the body absorb calcium and other minerals. Eat it straight from the pot or add it to your cereal, mix it with muesli, toss it with fruit or add to desserts.

Getting started

Remember that how you prepare and cook foods can make a big difference to their nutritional qualities. I use methods you may not be familiar with, such as almost never peeling vegetables and always soaking whole grains (these methods are explained in more detail on pages 18–19 and 22–25).

What equipment do I need?

For prepping vegetables, buy a natural bristle vegetable scrubber because instead of peeling vegetables, you'll be scrubbing them. Make sure you also have an excellent-quality knife for all of the cutting and chopping. For cooking, you'll need a few good stainless steel saucepans and skillets, and some baking dishes (I avoid aluminium and nonstick as there are questions about their safety). For steaming vegetables, a metal steamer is essential. For pureeing the baby's food, as well as making smoothies, breadcrumbs, bean dips and salsa, you'll need a small blender or food processor.

Keeping it clean

From 6 months old, I believe a little exposure to germs is a good thing. Babies who grow up in sterile environments have difficulty fighting infections and everyday colds. I don't bother with harsh, germ-killing cleaners because I don't want them around my family and I don't want to put them into the environment. I'm more afraid of the toxins in cleaners labeled with a skull and crossbones than I am of a few germs. Just make sure you always wash your hands before you cook, keep equipment clean, separate raw and cooked meats and cook eggs and meats thoroughly for young children.

Storing and freezing

Ceramic, glass or metal storage containers with lids are ideal for freezing the baby's food cubes. I stay away from plastic whenever possible because it contains harmful chemicals and pretty much never biodegrades. Any remaining food can be cooled, spooned into ice cube trays and frozen. When the cubes are solid, pop them out into another container, which you can date and label and store in the freezer for up to 3 months. You will soon build up a great selection of fruits, vegetables, grains, fish and meat from which you can pick and choose, either for a whole meal or to supplement something you have made fresh.

Food cubes quickly defrost and can be warmed in a small saucepan. Remember to defrost fish, poultry and meat in the refrigerator, and reheat rice thoroughly. You'll find the best way to feed your baby a good balance of different types of food is by cooking extra and freezing any leftovers. You can then add to any of the variations in the recipes with something from your freezer.

Steaming vegetables

It is best not to peel almost all vegetables, because of the nutrients and fiber in and just beneath the skin. And unless eating raw, it is best to steam vegetables rather than boil them. And for babies, steaming is

Kombu helps soften beans, reduces the cooking time and makes them easier to digest. It can also be left in with the beans (except for babies) for added nutrition and flavor. Always add salt after beans have cooked, partly so you can separate the beans for the baby and partly because salt toughens the skins and inhibits the beans' cooking.

Other ideas

I've cooked for a long time, but no one ever told me this simple trick, which would have saved me making a number of mistakes and forgetting ingredients just because I was tired or distracted. When you have bought everything you need and are ready to cook, start by getting all of the ingredients out on the counter. Then prep your vegetables and such, as listed in the ingredients list. After that, follow the method. When you have completed the recipe, read back over the recipe and the ingredients list to make sure that you have followed every stage and used all the ingredients. It may save you from making frustrating mistakes.

Remember, if you can, to try and make food fun, too. If your child stops trying new things, make a game of it. Have them close their eyes and taste five or six different things. Remind them to try the foods with an open mind, not knowing what to expect or what the food might be. You can include something they really like in the selection.

I love cooking, but often I used to have no idea what to do for dinner. So, I now do two things. First, I write down what I'm making for dinner every night for a week and buy the ingredients for those dishes. Second, I have a list of meals that we love to eat regularly for lunch and dinner, otherwise, I forget and tend to repeat foods too often. Don't be afraid to have the same foods on certain days, to make it easier for yourself. For example, we always have an eggy brunch on Sunday and pizza on Sunday night (it's my day off and this is what my husband likes to cook).

I also like to take a specific day each week to prepare for the week ahead. It's a day I commit to cooking and baking. I like to bake bread, a sweet baked good and a bean dip at least. And I do this on my grocery shopping day.

excellent. When you boil vegetables, a lot of the goodness goes into the water and is poured down the drain.

Pour water into a saucepan to a depth of ½-inch and bring to a boil. Put the vegetables in a steamer, put the steamer in the pan, cover and then steam about 5 minutes until just tender, but with a little crunch. For babies, steam the vegetables about 10 minutes (carrots 20 minutes and squash 30 minutes) until they are completely soft.

Soaking and cooking beans

Soaking beans in plenty of acidulated warm water (water with 1 tablespoon of lemon juice or vinegar) is an important step in their preparation. After they have soaked at least 12 hours, rinse the beans well, boil hard in fresh water 10 minutes, skimming any scum that rises to the surface, then cover and simmer with kombu (see page 17) until they are tender. This process ensures that the phytic acid will be neutralized, the beans will be easily digested, the nutrients will be released and the difficult-to-digest complex sugars will be broken down.

Ages & stages

6 to 9 months

When your baby is ready to wean, start with the foods from the list below. Your baby may have some teeth now, but all foods should be pureed until completely smooth. Add water if necessary when pureeing, so that the texture of all foods is the consistency of yogurt.

If your baby is chewing, slowly add some finely grated raw fruits and vegetables (you can include skins, because they will be either pureed or finely grated). Give your baby breast milk or formula for breakfast and then only between meals, to encourage eating at mealtimes. You can now offer a little warm, filtered water with lunch and dinner.

Include 2 teaspoons of seed oil a day, alternating with olive oil.

At this age you can introduce fish, poultry and meats, although in small quantities. You can also bring in oats. Historically, oats were harvested, transported and processed by machines that handle grains containing gluten, so many people with gluten allergies kept away from them. When isolated, oats do not have gluten (they do contain a glutenlike protein that only very sensitive people react to). Buy gluten-free oats that are uncontaminated as they can be included in foods for 6 to 9 month old babies. Ideally, oats should always be soaked with yogurt or kefir (see page 22).

It's difficult to eat fish that is not overfished, as the list of species in danger changes regularly. I recommend anchovies (only fresh), mackerel (not King), salmon (wild or organic farmed) and sardines because they are oily fish and have a lot of goodness. There are a few things to remember. Eat a variety—it wouldn't be good to feed your baby salmon all of the time, for example. And look for line-caught fish if you can find it. Avoid farmed fish, unless it is farmed organically—fish farming takes place under intensive conditions with the use of organophosphates, chlorine, antibiotics and other chemicals that are not good for your baby, you, the water or the land.

9 to 12 months

Your baby should be able to chew a little now, so food can be lumpier, you can add grated fruit or vegetables and you can serve little pieces (¼-inch) of fruit or vegetables, which will also encourage self-feeding. Make sure you sit with a baby who is eating small pieces of food in case he or she chokes. If your baby still isn't chewing much, don't worry and just continue to puree foods so that they will be properly digested.

Now come fruits with small seeds, some of the tougher, more fibrous vegetables and sprouts, which offer excellent

Foods to introduce at 6 to 9 months

- amaranth
- anchovy, fresh
- apple
- apricot
- artichoke heart
- avocado
- banana
- beef and red meats
- beet
- black (turtle) bean
- black-eyed pea
- broccoli
- buckwheat
- butternut squash
- cannellini bean
- carrot
- cauliflower

- celeriac
- cherry
- chickpea
- coconut
- fava bean
- flageolet bean
- flaxseed oil
- green bean
- hemp seed oil
- kefir, for soaking
- kombu, for cooking
- lemon juice, for soaking
- lentils (red, brown, large green, Puy)
- mackerel, not King
- mango
- millet

- mung bean
- navy bean
- nectarine
- oats (gluten-free)
- olive oil
- papaya
- parsnip
- pea
- peach
- pear
- pinto bean
- plum
- poultry
- prune
- pumpkin
- pumpkin seed oil
- quinoa

- rice (basmati, black, brown short/long-grain, brown sushi, jasmine, red Camargue, wild)
- rutabaga
- safflower oil
- salmon
- sardine
- sesame oil
- snow pea
- sunflower oil
- sweet potato
- turnip
- venison and game
- yogurt, for soaking
- zucchini

Foods to introduce at 9 to 12 months

- asparagus
- bok choy
- blackberry
- blueberry
- butter
- Chinese cabbage
- cornstarch/cornmeal
- cranberry, unsweetened
- cucumber
- currant (dried)

- date
- fennel
- fig
- fresh herbs, such as basil, mint and parsley
- garlic
- grape
- haddock
- Jerusalem artichoke

- kefir
- kiwi
- leek
- lychee
- oats
- onion
- napa leaf
- polenta
- pollock
- raisin

- raspberry
- rhubarb
- scallion
- sprouts (all types, including alfalfa, broccoli, chickpea, lentil, mung and radish)
- trout
- yogurt

nutrition. You can now also introduce plain yogurt and small amounts of butter. Carry on with 2 teaspoons of seed and/or olive oil per day.

From 12 months on

At 12 months your child can eat all family meals. You can offer strawberries and citrus in small quantities. It is also okay now to start with the deadly nightshade family (eggplant, mushroom, potato, tomato and sweet pepper) and some gluten-containing grains. Egg and soy can be introduced, keeping soy products to a minimum and favoring tempeh over soy.

You can go ahead with wheat (although keeping it to a minimum is a good idea), nuts (except peanuts until 5 years) and seeds are allowed—just make sure they are being chewed well—and organic cheese can be eaten, focusing on cheese from sheep and goats in preference to cheese from cows.

As well as continuing with 2 teaspoons of seed or olive oil per day, you can make an essential fatty acid (EFA) seed mix. Put 1 measure each of sesame seeds and your choice of either sunflower or pumpkin seeds in a jar. Add 2 measures of flax seeds, seal tightly and keep in the refrigerator away from light, heat and air. Grind 1 teaspoon of the mixture in a spice mill or coffee grinder at mealtimes and mix it with your child's food. You can alternate this with the oils.

From 12 months, your child can eat everything, including:

- almond
- arugula
- barley
- bell pepper (red, yellow, orange, green)
- Brazil nut
- Brussels sprout
- cabbage
- caper
- cashew nut
- celery
- cheese, especially from organic goat and sheep milk
- chestnut
- clementine
- corn

- edamame bean
- eggplant
- eggs
- flaxseeds, ground
- grapefruit
- hazelnut
- hemp seeds, ground
- kale
- Kamut
- kumquat
- lemon
- lettuce
- lime
- macadamia nut
- mandarin
- mushroom
- olives, pitted

- orange
- passion fruit
- pecan
- pickle
- pine nut
- pistachio nut
- pomegranate
- pomelo
- potato
- pumpkin seeds, ground
- rye
- samphire
- satsuma
- seaweed (arame, hijiki, kombu, nori)
- sesame seeds, ground

- soy, including tempeh and tofu
- spelt
- spinach
- strawberry
- sunflower seeds, ground
- Swiss chard
- tangelo
- tangerine
- tomato
- walnut
- watercress
- wheat

Basic recipes

These pages contain all of the basic recipes for cooking grains and beans. Because you may be using these recipes often, you might want to photocopy these pages —or the one you use the most—and stick them on your refrigerator or cupboard.

The methods say to soak grains and rice at least 7 hours. If you remember the night before, then put grains to soak then, because the extra soaking time will only be an improvement. If, however, you forget, then you still have time to put something to soak in the morning for a meal you are cooking that evening. If you don't remember until the afternoon, make the meal anyway, but do try to get into the excellent habit of soaking grains.

The recipe cooking times that follow are for adults. You must add on 20 minutes if you are cooking any grains for your baby and add an extra ½ cup warm water to the saucepan. Rice for an adult should be cooked until it retains a slight bite, but for babies, should be completely soft.

If these recipes require seasoning, then add 1 teaspoon of fine sea salt for each 1 cup of uncooked grain or bean.

GRAINS

COOKED MILLET

PREPARATION: 5 minutes, plus at least 7 hours soaking
COOKING TIME: 20 minutes

½ cup millet
½ teaspoon plain yogurt or kefir

1 Put the millet, yogurt and 2 cups warm water in a saucepan and let soak, covered, 7 hours or overnight at room temperature.

2 Bring to a boil over high heat, then turn the heat down to low and simmer, covered, 20 minutes until soft.

COOKED BUCKWHEAT

PREPARATION: 5 minutes, plus at least 7 hours soaking
COOKING TIME: 20 minutes

⅓ cup buckwheat
1 tablespoon plain yogurt or kefir

1 Put the buckwheat, yogurt and scant 1⅓ cups warm water in a saucepan and let soak, covered, 7 hours or overnight at room temperature.

2 Bring to a boil over high heat, then turn the heat down to low and simmer, covered, 20 minutes until completely soft.

COOKED OATMEAL

PREPARATION: 5 minutes, plus at least 7 hours soaking
COOKING TIME: 10 minutes

1 cup rolled oats
1 tablespoon plain yogurt or kefir

1 Put the oats, yogurt and 3¼ cups warm water in a saucepan and let soak, covered, 7 hours or overnight at room temperature.

2 Bring to a simmer over medium heat, then turn the heat down to low and simmer, stirring occasionally, 10 minutes until soft and creamy.

COOKED QUINOA OR RED QUINOA

PREPARATION: 5 minutes, plus at least 7 hours soaking
COOKING TIME: 20 minutes

1 cup quinoa or red quinoa
1 tablespoon plain yogurt or kefir

1 Put the quinoa, yogurt and 3¼ cups warm water in a saucepan and let soak, covered, 7 hours or overnight at room temperature.

2 Bring to a boil over high heat, then turn the heat down to low and simmer, covered, 20 minutes until tender.

COOKED BROWN BASMATI RICE

PREPARATION: 5 minutes, plus at least 7 hours soaking
COOKING TIME: 35 minutes

1 cup brown basmati rice
1 tablespoon plain yogurt or kefir

1 Put the rice, yogurt and 2 cups warm water in a saucepan and let soak, covered, 7 hours or overnight at room temperature.

2 Bring to a boil over high heat, then turn the heat down to low and simmer, covered, 35 minutes until the rice is just cooked but still retains a slight bite.

COOKED BROWN RICE, BROWN SUSHI RICE OR BROWN SHORT-GRAIN RICE, RED CAMARGUE RICE

PREPARATION: 5 minutes, plus at least 7 hours soaking
COOKING TIME: 40 minutes

1 cup brown rice, brown sushi rice or brown short-grain rice, red Camargue rice
1 tablespoon plain yogurt or kefir

1 Put the rice, yogurt and 2 cups warm water in a saucepan and let soak, covered, 7 hours or overnight at room temperature.

2 Bring to a boil over high heat, then turn the heat down to low and simmer, covered, 40 minutes until the rice is just cooked but still retains a slight bite.

COOKED WILD RICE

PREPARATION: 5 minutes, plus at least 7 hours soaking
COOKING TIME: 40 minutes

½ cup wild rice
½ tablespoon plain yogurt or kefir

1 Put the wild rice, yogurt and generous 1 cup warm water in a saucepan and let soak, covered, 7 hours or overnight at room temperature.

2 Bring to a boil over high heat, then turn the heat down to low and simmer, covered, 40 minutes until the rice is just cooked but still retains a slight bite.

DRIED BEANS & LENTILS

COOKED DRIED BLACK BEANS

PREPARATION: 5 minutes, plus at least 12 hours soaking
COOKING TIME: 1 hour 40 minutes

½ cup black (turtle) beans
½ tablespoon lemon juice, grape vinegar or white wine vinegar
½ strip of kombu, about 3¼ x 2 inches (optional)

1 Put the black beans in a saucepan. Add the lemon juice, cover generously with warm water and let soak, covered, 12 hours or overnight at room temperature.

2 Drain and rinse the beans, then return them to the pan. Add generous 1½ cups water and bring to a boil over high heat. Boil 10 minutes, skimming any scum that rises to the surface, then turn the heat down to low and add the kombu, if using. Simmer, covered, 1½ hours until soft. Check occasionally to make sure that the beans remain covered with water and add extra boiling water if necessary. Remove the kombu from the pan and reserve for chopping or mashing. Drain the beans.

COOKED DRIED CANNELLINI BEANS

PREPARATION: 5 minutes, plus at least 12 hours soaking
COOKING TIME: 1 hour 10 minutes

½ cup dried cannellini beans
½ tablespoon lemon juice, grape vinegar or white wine vinegar
½ strip of kombu, about 3¼ x 2 inches (optional)

1 Put the cannellini beans in a saucepan. Add the lemon juice, cover generously with warm water and let soak, covered, 12 hours or overnight at room temperature.

2 Drain and rinse the beans, then return them to the pan. Add 5 cups water and bring to a boil over high heat. Boil 10 minutes, skimming any scum that rises to the surface, then turn the heat down to low and add the kombu, if using. Simmer, covered, 1 hour until soft. Check occasionally to make sure that the beans remain covered with water and add extra boiling water if necessary. Remove the kombu from the pan and reserve for chopping or mashing. Drain the beans.

COOKED DRIED CHICKPEAS

PREPARATION: 5 minutes, plus at least 12 hours soaking
COOKING TIME: 2 hours 10 minutes

½ **cup dried chickpeas**
½ **tablespoon lemon juice, grape vinegar or white wine vinegar**
½ **strip of kombu, about 3¼ x 2 inches (optional)**

1 Put the chickpeas in a saucepan. Add the lemon juice, cover generously with warm water and let soak, covered, 12 hours or overnight at room temperature.

2 Drain and rinse the chickpeas, then return them to the pan. Add 6 cups water and bring to a boil over high heat. Boil 10 minutes, skimming any scum that rises to the surface, then turn the heat down to low and add the kombu, if using. Simmer, covered, 2 hours until soft. Check occasionally to make sure that the chickpeas remain covered with water and add extra boiling water if necessary. Remove the kombu from the pan and reserve for chopping or mashing. Drain the chickpeas.

COOKED DRIED NAVY BEANS

PREPARATION: 5 minutes, plus at least 12 hours soaking
COOKING TIME: 1 hour 40 minutes

1 **cup navy beans**
1 **tablespoon lemon juice, grape vinegar or white wine vinegar**
1 **strip of kombu, 6¼ x 4 inches (optional)**

1 Put the navy beans in a saucepan. Add the lemon juice, cover generously with warm water and let soak, covered, 12 hours or overnight at room temperature.

2 Drain and rinse the beans, then return them to the pan. Add 5 cups water and bring to a boil over high heat. Boil 10 minutes, skimming any scum that rises to the surface, then turn the heat down to low and add the kombu, if using. Simmer, covered, 1½ hours until soft. Check occasionally to make sure that the beans remain covered with water and add extra boiling water if necessary. Remove the kombu from the pan and reserve for chopping or mashing. Drain the beans.

COOKED DRIED KIDNEY BEANS

PREPARATION: 5 minutes, plus at least 12 hours soaking
COOKING TIME: 1 hour 40 minutes

1 **cup kidney beans**
1 **tablespoon lemon juice, grape vinegar or white wine vinegar**
1 **strip of kombu, 6¼ x 4 inches (optional)**

1 Put the kidney beans in a saucepan. Add the lemon juice, cover generously with warm water and let soak, covered, 12 hours or overnight at room temperature.

2 Drain and rinse the beans, then return them to the pan. Add 4⅓ cups water and bring to a boil over high heat. Boil 10 minutes, skimming any scum that rises to the surface, then turn the heat down to low and add the kombu, if using. Simmer, covered, 1½ hours until soft. Check occasionally to make sure that the beans remain covered with water and add extra boiling water if necessary. Remove the kombu from the pan and reserve for chopping or mashing. Drain the beans.

COOKED MUNG BEANS

PREPARATION: 5 minutes, plus at least 12 hours soaking
COOKING TIME: 55 minutes

½ cup mung beans
½ tablespoon lemon juice, grape vinegar or white wine vinegar
½ strip of kombu, about 3¼ x 2 inches (optional)

1 Put the mung beans in a saucepan. Add the lemon juice, cover generously with warm water and let soak, covered, 12 hours or overnight at room temperature.

2 Drain and rinse the beans, then return them to the pan. Add 3¼ cups water and bring to a boil over high heat. Boil 10 minutes, skimming any scum that rises to the surface, then turn the heat down to low and add the kombu, if using. Simmer, covered, 45 minutes until soft. Check occasionally to make sure that the beans remain covered with water and add extra boiling water if necessary. Remove the kombu from the pan and reserve for chopping or mashing. Drain the beans.

COOKED DRIED PINTO BEANS

PREPARATION: 5 minutes, plus at least 12 hours soaking
COOKING TIME: 1 hour 40 minutes

1 cup pinto beans
1½ tablespoons lemon juice, grape vinegar or white wine vinegar
1 strip of kombu, 6¼ x 4 inches (optional)

1 Put the pinto beans in a saucepan. Add the lemon juice, cover generously with warm water and let soak, covered, 12 hours or overnight at room temperature.

2 Drain and rinse the beans, then return them to the pan. Add 6½ cups water and bring to a boil over high heat. Boil 10 minutes, skimming any scum that rises to the surface, then turn the heat down to low and add the kombu, if using. Simmer, covered, 1½ hours until soft. Check occasionally to make sure that the beans remain covered with water and add extra boiling water if necessary. Remove the kombu from the pan and reserve for chopping or mashing. Drain the beans.

COOKED LARGE GREEN LENTILS

PREPARATION: 5 minutes, plus at least 12 hours soaking
COOKING TIME: 30 minutes

1 cup large green lentils
1 tablespoon lemon juice, grape vinegar or white wine vinegar
1 strip of kombu, 6¼ x 4 inches (optional)

1 Put the lentils in a saucepan. Add the lemon juice, cover generously with warm water and let soak, covered, 12 hours or overnight at room temperature.

2 Drain and rinse the lentils, then return them to the pan. Add 3¼ cups water and bring to a boil over high heat, then turn the heat down to low and add the kombu to the pan, if using. Simmer, covered, 30 minutes until soft and starting to break up. Remove the kombu from the pan and reserve for chopping or mashing. Drain the lentils.

SOAKED BROWN OR PUY LENTILS

PREPARATION: 5 minutes, plus at least 7 hours soaking

1 cup brown lentils or Puy lentils
1 tablespoon lemon juice, grape vinegar or white wine vinegar

1 Put the lentils in a saucepan. Add the lemon juice, cover generously with warm water and let soak, covered, 7 hours or overnight at room temperature. Drain and rinse the lentils.

chapter one
start the day well

I love breakfast because it's a brilliant opportunity to get something wonderful into your baby or your kids, as everyone usually wakes up hungry. There are recipes here for rushed mornings when you're short on time, like the Pear & Pecan Smoothie. This recipe then gives you a Pear & Brown Rice Puree for a 6 to 9 month old and Pear, Rice & Yogurt Mix for a 9 to 12 month old.

For mornings when you have planned ahead, there are lovely soaked hot cereals made from fabulous grains like amaranth or millet. And for the leisurely weekends when you get up with nowhere you have to be, you can mix up some Three-Grain Pancakes with Papaya. Forget those sugary breakfast cereals and discover wonderful dishes to start the day well. You'll also find breakfast breads in chapter four.

Mixing up a smoothie in the blender is an easy way to make breakfast quickly. The pecans add protein, essential oil and a creamy richness. And it's easier to get some children to eat fruit if it's pureed into a yummy drink.

Pear & Pecan Smoothie

SERVES: 2 adults, 1 child and 1 baby
PREPARATION TIME: 5 minutes
STORAGE: Refrigerate up to 3 days.

. . . .

2 large pears, cored and coarsely chopped
heaped ⅓ cup pecans
2 cups oat milk, or rice milk
⅔ cup plain yogurt
6 tablespoons instant baby wholegrain rice flakes

1 Put all of the ingredients in a blender and blend 30 seconds until smooth. Pour into glasses and serve.

6-9 PEAR & BROWN RICE PUREE
Put 9 pear pieces, 3 tablespoons of the rice flakes and ½ cup water in a blender. Blend 30 seconds, adding extra water 1 teaspoon at a time, until smooth. Serve warm or at room temperature.

9-12 PEAR, RICE & YOGURT MIX
Put 9 pear pieces, 2 tablespoons of the rice flakes, 2 tablespoons of the yogurt and ¼ cup water in a blender. Pulse 15 seconds, adding extra water 1 teaspoon at a time, until the mixture forms a lumpy puree. Serve warm or at room temperature.

This is great for kids—or when you have guests to stay. Combined with fresh or dried fruit, nuts and seeds, the yogurt mixture is nourishing and sustaining. Put a selection of ingredients out for everyone to sprinkle in their bowl and create their own flavor combinations.

Fruit & Nut Medley with Yogurt

SERVES: 2 adults, 1 child and 1 baby
PREPARATION TIME: 10 minutes
STORAGE: Refrigerate up to 3 days.

....

1¼ cup raisins
2 nectarines, pitted and chopped
heaped ⅓ cup ground almonds
4 tablespoons dried coconut
4 teaspoons sunflower seeds
4 teaspoons flaxseeds
2 cups plain yogurt

1 Put the raisins and scant ⅔ cup boiling water in a heatproof bowl and let soften 5 minutes.

2 (6-9) (9-12) Put the nectarines, ground almonds, coconut and seeds in a large bowl. Drain the raisins and discard the soaking water, then add them to the bowl and mix in. Add the yogurt, mix well and serve.

(6-9) **NECTARINE PUREE**
Put ¼ of the nectarines and 2 tablespoons water in a blender. Blend 30 seconds, adding extra water 1 teaspoon at a time, until smooth. Serve warm or at room temperature.

(9-12) **NECTARINE, RAISIN & YOGURT MIX**
Put ¼ of the nectarines, 1 tablespoon of the soaked raisins, 2 tablespoons of the yogurt and 1 tablespoon water in a blender. Pulse 15 seconds, adding extra water 1 teaspoon at a time, until the mixture forms a lumpy puree. Serve warm or at room temperature.

I love soaking muesli with yogurt because it becomes very creamy. It also makes muesli more digestible and means that the minerals in the muesli, such as iron, magnesium, calcium and zinc are absorbed more easily by your body. You can double this recipe and store the dried mix in a jar.

Swiss Muesli

SERVES: 2 adults, 1 child and 1 baby
PREPARATION TIME: 20 minutes, plus overnight soaking
STORAGE: Refrigerate soaked muesli up to 3 days.

....

1½ cups rolled oats
½ cup millet (or any other grain) flakes
¼ cup raisins
¼ cup dried cranberries
2 tablespoons flaked almonds
2 tablespoons coarsely chopped hazelnuts
2 tablespoons sunflower seeds
2 tablespoons flaxseeds
3 tablespoons plain yogurt or kefir
1 apple

1 (6-9) (9-12) Mix the oats, millet flakes, raisins, cranberries, almonds, hazelnuts and seeds in a large bowl. Add the yogurt and 2⅔ cups warm water and mix well. Let soak, covered, overnight at room temperature.

2 Core and grate the apple, then mix into the muesli and serve.

(6-9) OAT & APPLE PUREE
Put 4 tablespoons of the oats, ½ teaspoon of the yogurt and ¾ cup warm water in a saucepan and let soak, covered, overnight at room temperature. Bring to a simmer over medium heat, then turn the heat down to low and cook, stirring occasionally, 10 minutes until completely soft. Transfer to a blender and add ½ of the grated apple and 2 tablespoons water. Blend 30 seconds, adding extra water 1 teaspoon at a time, until smooth. Serve warm.

 FRUIT & OAT MIX
Put 4 tablespoons of the oats, 1 teaspoon of the raisins, 1 teaspoon of the cranberries, 1 teaspoon of the yogurt and ¾ cup warm water in a saucepan and let soak, covered, overnight at room temperature. Bring to a simmer over medium heat, then turn the heat down to low and cook, stirring occasionally, 10 minutes until completely soft. Transfer to a blender and add 2 tablespoons water. Pulse 15 seconds, adding extra water 1 teaspoon at a time, until the mixture forms a lumpy puree. Mix 1 tablespoon of the grated apple into the oat mixture and serve warm.

Dried mango adds a lovely sweetness and a host of wonderful nutrients to this breakfast. It's worth slotting amaranth into your repertoire of grains and breakfasts: it's a good source of protein and an excellent source of calcium—which you and your kids need.

Amaranth with Mango

SERVES: 2 adults, 1 child and 1 baby
PREPARATION TIME: 10 minutes, plus at least 7 hours soaking (optional)
COOKING TIME: 40 minutes
STORAGE: Refrigerate up to 3 days.

. . . .

½ cup amaranth
2½ tablespoons plain yogurt or kefir (optional)
¼ cup dried mango, chopped

1 (9-12) If soaking the amaranth, put the amaranth, yogurt and generous 2½ cups warm water in a large saucepan. Add the mango and mix well. Let soak, covered, 7 hours or overnight at room temperature.

2 Bring to a boil over high heat. Turn the heat down to low and cook, covered, 40 minutes, stirring occasionally, until the amaranth is completely soft and cooked through.

(If cooking unsoaked amaranth, put the amaranth and generous 2½ cups water in a large saucepan. Mix in the mango and bring to a boil over high heat. Turn the heat down to low and cook, covered, 40 minutes, stirring occasionally, until the amaranth is completely soft and cooked through.)

3 (6-9) Remove from the heat and serve warm.

(6-9)

AMARANTH & MANGO PUREE
Put 4 tablespoons of the cooked amaranth and mango mixture and 2 tablespoons water in a blender. Blend 30 seconds, adding extra water 1 teaspoon at a time, until smooth. Serve warm.

(9-12)

AMARANTH, MANGO & YOGURT MIX
Put 4 tablespoons of the cooked amaranth and mango mixture, 2 tablespoons of the yogurt and 1 tablespoon water in a blender. Pulse 15 seconds, adding extra water 1 teaspoon at a time, until the mixture forms a lumpy puree. Serve warm.

When I first made this, my husband Brian pulled a face and reached for the muesli instead. But when he tried it, he loved the combination of creamy millet and crunchy nuts with the sweetness of dates and rice malt syrup.

Millet Simmer with Dates & Hazelnuts

SERVES: 2 adults, 1 child and 1 baby
PREPARATION TIME: 10 minutes, plus at least 7 hours soaking and 20 minutes cooking the millet
STORAGE: Refrigerate up to 3 days.

¼ cup hazelnuts
1 recipe quantity cooked millet (see page 22)
½ cup plain yogurt
4 dates, pitted and finely chopped
3 tablespoons rice malt syrup or 2½ tablespoons cane sugar

1 Put the hazelnuts in a plastic bag and break into small pieces with a rolling pin. Transfer to a bowl, add the cooked millet, yogurt, dates and rice malt syrup and mix until warmed through, then serve.

6-9 MILLET HOT CEREAL PUREE
Put 4 tablespoons of the cooked millet and generous ½ cup boiling water in a saucepan and simmer, covered, over low heat 20 minutes until completely soft. Transfer to a blender and add 2 tablespoons water. Blend 30 seconds, adding extra water 1 teaspoon at a time, until smooth. Serve warm.

9-12 MILLET & DATE HOT CEREAL
Put 4 tablespoons of the cooked millet, ½ tablespoon of the dates and generous ½ cup boiling water in a saucepan and simmer, covered, over low heat 20 minutes until completely soft. Transfer to a blender and add 2 tablespoons water. Pulse 15 seconds, adding extra water 1 teaspoon at a time, until the mixture forms a lumpy puree. Serve warm.

On weekends when you have a little more time, this is a lovely breakfast treat. With a crispy crust on the outside and delicate dough on the inside, it's a favorite with everyone. My kids love it because they feel like they're having pie for breakfast.

Baked Apple Puff

SERVES: 2 adults, 1 child and 1 baby
PREPARATION TIME: 15 minutes
COOKING TIME: 25 minutes
STORAGE: Store in an airtight container up to 2 days.

. . . .

3 extra-large eggs
scant ⅔ cup oat milk, rice milk or water
½ cup wholegrain spelt flour or wholewheat flour
2½ tablespoons rice malt syrup or 2 tablespoons cane sugar
½ teaspoon vanilla extract
1 teaspoon ground cinnamon
¼ teaspoon fine sea salt
1 tablespoon unsalted butter
2 apples, cored and thinly sliced

1 Preheat the oven to 400°F. In a large mixing bowl, lightly beat the eggs together with a whisk. **(9-12)** Add the oat milk, flour, rice malt syrup, vanilla extract, cinnamon and salt and whisk until smooth.

2 Melt the butter in a 10-inch flameproof pie plate in the oven. Remove from the oven and tilt the pie plate to evenly coat the bottom in melted butter. **(6-9)** Pour the batter into the pie plate and arrange the apples on top. Bake 25 minutes until lightly browned. Serve warm.

(6-9) BAKED APPLE PUREE
Chop 10 apple slices into small pieces. Put the apple and 1 tablespoon water in a small ramekin and bake as above 15 minutes until the apple is completely soft. Transfer to a blender and blend 30 seconds, adding water 1 teaspoon at a time, until smooth. Serve warm.

(9-12) BAKED CINNAMON APPLE
Chop 10 apple slices into small pieces. Put the apple, 1 tablespoon of the oat milk, 1 teaspoon of the melted butter and a pinch of the cinnamon in a small ramekin and bake as above 15 minutes until the apple is completely soft. Transfer to a blender and pulse 15 seconds, adding water 1 teaspoon at a time, until the mixture forms a lumpy puree. Serve warm.

Saturday pancakes are a family tradition. I like to mix the oat milk, grains and yogurt the night before and let them stand at room temperature to ferment a little. In the morning, just mix in the other ingredients.

Three-Grain Pancakes with Papaya

MAKES: 12 pancakes
PREPARATION TIME: 20 minutes
COOKING TIME: 18 minutes
STORAGE: Refrigerate the uncooked batter for up to 1 day. Refrigerate the pancakes up to 3 days.

....

1 papaya, peeled, seeded and coarsely chopped
1 extra-large egg
1 cup oat milk, rice milk or water
3 tablespoons sunflower oil, plus extra for frying if needed
⅓ cup buckwheat flour
¾ cup wholegrain spelt flour or wholewheat flour
⅓ cup instant polenta
1½ teaspoons baking powder
½ teaspoon fine sea salt
unsalted butter and maple syrup, to serve (optional), or 1 lemon, cut into wedges and cane sugar, to serve (optional)

1 Put the papaya in a blender and blend, adding water 1 tablespoon at a time, until smooth, then transfer to a bowl and set aside. (6-9) (9-18)

2 In a large bowl, lightly beat the egg with a whisk. Add the oat milk and 1 tablespoon of the oil and whisk. In another bowl, mix together the flours, polenta, baking powder and salt. Add the flour mixture to the egg mixture and whisk until smooth.

3 Preheat the oven to 200°F. Heat the remaining oil in a large, heavy-bottomed skillet, or heat a griddle pan, over medium-low heat. Working in batches, pour 2 tablespoons of the batter into the skillet to make a pancake and repeat, spacing the pancakes slightly apart. Cook 2 to 3 minutes on each side or until the bubbles that appear on the surface pop and the undersides of the pancakes are lightly browned. Keep warm in the oven while you repeat with the remaining batter, adding more oil to the skillet as needed.

4 Serve hot with the papaya puree. Alternatively, serve with a little butter spread on top and some maple syrup drizzled over, or sprinkle with freshly squeezed lemon juice and sugar.

(6-9) PAPAYA PUREE
Put 5 tablespoons of the papaya puree in a bowl and serve warm or at room temperature.

(9-18) BUCKWHEAT PANCAKES WITH PAPAYA PUREE
Mix together 2 tablespoons of the buckwheat flour and 3 tablespoons water in a small bowl to form a smooth paste. Heat 1 tablespoon of the oil in a heavy-bottomed skillet over medium-low heat. Pour the batter into the skillet to make a pancake and cook 1 to 2 minutes on each side until the bubbles that appear on the surface pop and the underside of the pancake is lightly browned. Transfer to a blender and add 2 tablespoons water. Pulse 15 seconds, adding extra water 1 teaspoon at a time, until the mixture forms a lumpy puree. Serve warm with 2 tablespoons of the papaya puree.

When you've got bananas that are getting old, either make these simple hotcakes or Banana Walnut Bread (see page 143). Great just with butter, these are naturally sweet and satisfying. Loved by young and old, bananas are an excellent source of potassium, an essential mineral.

Banana Hotcakes

MAKES: 12
PREPARATION TIME: 15 minutes
COOKING TIME: 18 minutes
STORAGE: Use the same day.

. . . .

2 extra-large eggs
4 bananas
2 tablespoons plain yogurt
⅔ cup wholegrain spelt flour or wholewheat flour
½ cup rolled oats
1 teaspoon baking powder
2 tablespoons unsalted butter, plus extra for frying if needed and to serve

1 In a small bowl, lightly beat the eggs together with a whisk. (9-12) In a large mixing bowl, mash the bananas, using a fork, until smooth. (6-9) Add the eggs, yogurt, flour, oats and baking powder and mix until well combined.

2 Heat a large, heavy-bottomed skillet, or griddle pan, over medium-low heat until hot. Add the butter and heat until melted, tilting the skillet to evenly coat the bottom. Working in batches, pour 2 tablespoons of the batter into the skillet and repeat, spacing the hotcakes slightly apart. Cook 2 to 3 minutes on each side until lightly browned. Repeat with the remaining batter, adding more butter to the skillet as needed. Serve warm with a little butter spread on top.

(6-9) OAT & BANANA PUREE
Put 4 tablespoons of the oats, 1 teaspoon of the yogurt and ¾ cup warm water in a saucepan and let soak, covered, 7 hours or overnight at room temperature. Bring to a boil over high heat, then turn the heat down to low and, simmer, covered, 10 minutes, stirring occasionally, until completely soft. Put the oatmeal, 2 tablespoons of the mashed banana and 2 tablespoons water in a blender. Blend 30 seconds, adding extra water 1 teaspoon at a time, until smooth. Serve warm.

(9-12) FRIED BANANA COINS
Slice ½ of 1 banana into thick coins. Heat 1 teaspoon of the butter in a skillet over medium heat until melted. Add the bananas and fry 3 minutes on each side until the bananas are completely soft and lightly browned. Serve warm.

This nutrient-packed breakfast combines protein with complex carbohydrates and fresh fruit. Very quick to make, they will nourish and sustain you through the morning. If I eat these when I'm up early with the kids, I don't feel my first tummy rumble until midday.

Fried Peach Fritters

MAKES: 12
PREPARATION TIME: 10 minutes, plus at least 7 hours soaking and 10 minutes cooking the oatmeal
COOKING TIME: 25 minutes
STORAGE: Refrigerate up to 3 days.

....

2 extra-large eggs
1 recipe quantity cooked oatmeal (see page 22)
3 tablespoons wholegrain spelt flour or wholewheat flour
2 peaches, pitted and finely chopped
½ teaspoon fine sea salt
2 tablespoons unsalted butter, plus extra for frying if needed

1 In a large mixing bowl, lightly beat the eggs together with a whisk. Add the cooked oatmeal, flour, peaches and salt and mix well.

2 Heat the butter in a large, heavy-bottomed skillet over medium-high heat until melted, tilting the skillet to evenly coat the bottom. Working in batches, pour 2 tablespoons of the batter into the skillet to make a fritter and repeat, spacing the fritters slightly apart. Cook 4 to 5 minutes on each side until the fritters are lightly browned and crisp around the edges. If they break as you try to lift them, give them another minute or so to cook. Repeat with the remaining batter, adding more butter to the skillet as needed. Serve hot.

 PEACH OATMEAL PUREE
Put ¼ of the peaches, 4 tablespoons of the cooked oatmeal and 2 tablespoons water in a blender. Blend 30 seconds, adding extra water 1 teaspoon at a time, until smooth. Serve warm.

9-12 FRIED PEACH OATMEAL
Put ¼ of the peaches and 4 tablespoons of the cooked oatmeal in a blender. Pulse 15 seconds until the mixture forms a lumpy puree. Heat 1 teaspoon of the butter in a skillet over medium heat until melted. Add the peach and oatmeal mixture and cook, stirring occasionally, 4 to 5 minutes until lightly browned. Serve warm.

Salmon and eggs are a winning combination. If you sleep in late after a difficult night or it's a lazy weekend for everyone, this is a great, protein-rich dish for you and your little one first thing. Toddlers and older children love eating out of their own little ramekin.

Mini Salmon Egg Bakes

MAKES: 6
PREPARATION TIME: 30 minutes
COOKING TIME: 18 minutes
STORAGE: Refrigerate up to 1 day.

....

extra virgin olive oil, for greasing
1 onion, finely chopped
5½ ounces boneless, skinless salmon
    fillets, coarsely chopped
6 extra-large eggs
1 tablespoon Dijon mustard
a large pinch of cayenne pepper
¼ teaspoon fine sea salt
freshly ground black pepper
buttered toast, to serve

1 Preheat the oven to 400°F and grease six ramekins with oil.

2 (6-9) (9-12) Divide the onion and salmon evenly into the ramekins and set aside. In a bowl, beat the eggs together with a whisk. Add the mustard, cayenne pepper and salt, season with pepper and mix well. Pour the egg mixture evenly into the ramekins.

3 Put the ramekins in a deep baking dish and fill the dish with enough boiling water to come halfway up the sides of the ramekins. Bake 15 to 18 minutes until firm to the touch and very lightly browned. Serve warm with buttered toast.

(6-9)

SALMON PUREE
Heat a skillet over medium-low heat until hot. Add 1¾ ounces of the salmon and 1 tablespoon water and cook, covered, 10 minutes until the salmon is opaque and completely cooked through. Transfer to a blender and add 2 tablespoons water. Blend 30 seconds, adding extra water 1 teaspoon at a time, until smooth. Serve warm.

(9-12)

SALMON & ONION MIX
Heat a skillet over medium-low heat until hot. Add 1¾ ounces of the salmon, 1 tablespoon of the onion and 1 tablespoon water. Cook, stirring occasionally, 10 minutes until the salmon is opaque and completely cooked through and the onion is soft. Transfer to a blender and add 2 tablespoons water. Pulse 15 seconds, adding extra water 1 teaspoon at a time, until the mixture forms a lumpy puree. Serve warm.

chapter two
time for lunch

Lunchtime is a great opportunity to take a little bit of time out of your hectic day and sit with your family. Here you'll find a wide selection of recipes to fill them with delicious, nourishing food—all easy to make, and all with variations for your baby.

Try the ingenious recipe for Chicken, Ham & Cheesy Pasta, for example. No need to make a separate cheese sauce, or to cook the vegetables first. What's more, you can quickly blend up a Chicken, Broccoli & Cauliflower Pasta Puree for a 6 to 9 month old, or a Chicken with Mixed Vegetables & Pasta for a 9 to 12 month old.

Lunches are wonderful eaten outdoors and sometimes need to be on the run. You'll find recipes that work for you—Corn Fritters with Ham & Mango Salsa and Bean Dip Feast, for example—both perfect for filling lunch bags or for picnics in the park or on the beach.

Wraps are fun because you can fill them with your favorite foods and take them with you—to the park, the beach or wherever you're heading. Tahini is made of ground sesame seeds that contain a wealth of nutrients, including calcium and zinc, which are great for building little bones.

Chicken & Tahini Wrap

MAKES: 6
PREPARATION TIME: 30 minutes
COOKING TIME: 5 minutes
STORAGE: Refrigerate up to 1 day.

....

3 tablespoons extra virgin olive oil
3 boneless, skinless chicken breasts or
    6 boneless, skinless chicken thighs,
    cut into small strips
2¾ ounces cauliflower, finely chopped
½ tablespoon chopped sage leaves
    or ½ teaspoon dried sage
¾ teaspoon fine sea salt
¼ teaspoon freshly ground black
    pepper
6 tablespoons tahini
6 wholewheat or multigrain tortilla
    wraps
3 carrots, grated
3 scallions, white part only, finely sliced
½ lettuce, chopped
2 ounces sprouts, such as alfalfa,
    broccoli or mung (optional)

1 (6-9) (9-12) Heat the oil in a large, heavy-bottomed skillet over medium-high heat. Add the chicken and cauliflower and cook, stirring occasionally, 4 to 5 minutes until the chicken is beginning to brown and is cooked through and the cauliflower is tender. Remove from the heat, add the sage, salt and pepper and mix well.

2 Spread 1 tablespoon of the tahini down the centre of each wrap and top with the cooked chicken and cauliflower, and the carrots, scallions, lettuce and sprouts, if using. Roll up the wraps, tucking in one end, and serve.

(6-9) CHICKEN & CAULIFLOWER PUREE
Put 4 tablespoons of the cooked chicken and cauliflower mixture and 3 tablespoons water in a blender. Blend 30 seconds, adding extra water 1 teaspoon at a time, until smooth. Mix in 1 teaspoon of the oil and serve warm.

(9-12) CHICKEN WITH CAULIFLOWER, CARROTS & SPROUTS
Put 2 tablespoons of the cooked chicken, 1 tablespoon each of the cooked cauliflower, carrots and sprouts, if using, and 3 tablespoons water in a blender. Pulse 15 seconds, adding extra water 1 teaspoon at a time, until the mixture forms a lumpy puree. Mix in 1 teaspoon of the oil and serve warm.

Burgers can be surprisingly healthy when you make them at home with wholewheat buns, lettuce, tomato and onion. You can also introduce wonderful extras such as herbs on the inside and gherkins on the outside.

Chicken Burgers

SERVES: 2 adults, 1 child and 1 baby
PREPARATION TIME: 20 minutes
COOKING TIME: 10 minutes
STORAGE: Refrigerate up to 1 day.

....

14 ounces ground chicken, ground lamb, ground pork or ground beef
1 small onion, finely chopped, plus ½ onion, thinly sliced into rings, to serve
1 teaspoon chopped rosemary leaves (if using ground chicken)
½ teaspoon fine sea salt
¼ teaspoon freshly ground black pepper
2 tablespoons extra virgin olive oil
mayonnaise, for spreading
3 wholewheat burger buns, halved horizontally
ketchup, for spreading
6 lettuce leaves
2 tomatoes, thinly sliced
3 pickles, sliced lengthwise

1 (6-9) (9-12) Put the chicken, onion, rosemary, salt and pepper in a large bowl and mix well. Using your hands, shape the mixture into 3 burgers, using about twice the mixture for the adult portions that you use for the child portion.

2 Heat the oil in a large, heavy-bottomed skillet over medium heat. Add the burgers to the skillet and cook 5 minutes on each side until lightly browned and cooked through.

3 Spread mayonnaise on one half of each burger bun and ketchup on the other and serve the burgers in the buns, topped with the onion rings, lettuce, tomatoes and pickles.

(6-9) **GROUND CHICKEN PUREE**
Heat 1 teaspoon of the oil in a heavy-bottomed skillet over medium heat. Add 4 tablespoons of the ground chicken and cook, stirring occasionally, 3 to 4 minutes until the chicken is lightly browned and completely cooked through. Transfer to a blender and add 3 tablespoons water. Blend 30 seconds, adding extra water 1 teaspoon at a time, until smooth. Serve warm.

(9-12) **GROUND CHICKEN & ONION**
Heat 1 teaspoon of the oil in a heavy-bottomed skillet over medium heat. Add 4 tablespoons of the ground chicken and 1 tablespoon of the chopped onion and cook, stirring occasionally, 3 to 4 minutes until the chicken is lightly browned and completely cooked through. Transfer to a blender and add 3 tablespoons water. Pulse 15 seconds, adding extra water 1 teaspoon at a time, until the mixture forms a lumpy puree. Serve warm.

My brother David gave me this favorite recipe of his. The combination of chicken, ham and cheese create wonderful, strong flavors. My friend Kate made it and said it was so good that she managed to get her son, Barny, to eat cauliflower.

Chicken, Ham & Cheesy Pasta

SERVES: 2 adults, 1 child and 1 baby
PREPARATION TIME: 25 minutes
COOKING TIME: 30 minutes
STORAGE: Refrigerate up to 1 day.

....

3 boneless, skinless chicken breasts or 6 boneless, skinless chicken thighs
1 tablespoon unsalted butter
3 ounces cauliflower, cut into small florets
3 ounces broccoli, cut into small florets
1 small green bell pepper, halved, seeded and chopped
1 small onion, finely chopped
1 garlic clove, crushed
2 tablespoons wholegrain spelt flour or wholewheat flour
3 ounces ham, diced
1 ounce sharp cheddar cheese, grated
1 ounce Parmesan cheese or Romano cheese, grated
1 tablespoon Dijon mustard
1 teaspoon fine sea salt
10½ ounces brown rice pasta, millet pasta, quinoa pasta or buckwheat pasta, any shape
freshly ground black pepper

1 Preheat the broiler to medium. Put the chicken on a baking sheet and broil 5 to 8 minutes on each side until cooked through and the juices run clear. Remove from the broiler and slice the chicken into thin slices. (6-9) (9-12)

2 Heat the butter in a large, heavy-bottomed skillet over medium-high heat. Add the cauliflower, broccoli, bell pepper, onion and garlic and cook 5 minutes until just cooked but crunchy. Stir in the flour, then add ¾ cup water and bring to a boil over medium-high heat. Cook about 5 minutes, stirring continuously, until the sauce thickens. Mix in the ham, cheeses, mustard and salt, and season with pepper.

3 Meanwhile, cook the pasta in plenty of boiling water, according to the package directions. Drain well, add to the cheesy sauce and mix well. Serve hot, topped with slices of chicken.

(6-9) CHICKEN, BROCCOLI & CAULIFLOWER PASTA PUREE
Put 3 pieces each of the cauliflower and broccoli in a steamer and steam, covered, 10 minutes until completely soft. Transfer to a blender and add 1¾ ounces of the cooked chicken, 2 tablespoons of chopped, cooked pasta (without the cheesy sauce) and 4 tablespoons water. Blend 30 seconds, adding extra water 1 teaspoon at a time, until smooth. Serve warm.

(9-12) CHICKEN WITH MIXED VEGETABLES & PASTA
Put 3 pieces each of the cauliflower and broccoli, 1 teaspoon of the onion and a pinch of the garlic in a steamer and steam, covered, 10 minutes until completely soft. Transfer to a blender and add 1¾ ounces of the cooked chicken, 2 tablespoons of chopped, cooked pasta (without the cheesy sauce) and 4 tablespoons water. Pulse 15 seconds, adding extra water 1 teaspoon at a time, until the mixture forms a lumpy puree. Serve warm.

These fritters are good on their own, but with the mango salsa, they are incredible. We created them last summer when my sister, Jan, was here with her three kids and her daughter Alli was asking for something to eat with the mango salsa I'd made.

Corn Fritters with Ham & Mango Salsa

MAKES: 12
PREPARATION TIME: 40 minutes
COOKING TIME: 30 minutes
STORAGE: Refrigerate the fritter batter up to 1 day. Refrigerate the fritters and salsa up to 3 days.

....

3 extra-large eggs
1½ cups wholegrain spelt flour or wholewheat flour
heaped ½ cup instant polenta
1½ teaspoons fine sea salt
5 tablespoons extra virgin olive oil, plus extra for frying if needed
1⅓ cups frozen corn kernels, defrosted
10½ ounces sliced ham
salad, to serve

FOR THE MANGO SALSA
2 ripe mangoes, peeled, pitted and chopped
7 ounces cherry tomatoes
1 small red onion, finely chopped
4 tablespoons lime juice

1 (6-9) (9-12) To make the salsa, put all of the ingredients in a blender and pulse 15 seconds until chunky.

2 In a large mixing bowl, lightly beat the eggs together with a whisk. Add the flour, polenta, salt, 3 tablespoons of the oil and ¾ cup water and whisk. Add the corn kernels and mix well.

3 Heat the remaining oil in a large, heavy-bottomed skillet over medium-low heat. Working in batches, pour 2 tablespoons of the batter into the skillet to make a fritter and repeat, spacing the fritters slightly apart. Cook 4 to 5 minutes on each side or until lightly browned. Repeat with the remaining batter, adding more oil to the skillet as needed. Top each fritter with sliced ham and a tablespoon of the salsa and serve warm with salad.

(6-9) HAM & MANGO PUREE
Put 1¾ ounces of the ham, 2 tablespoons of the mango and 3 tablespoons water in a blender. Blend 30 seconds, adding extra water 1 teaspoon at a time, until smooth. Mix in 1 teaspoon of the oil and serve warm.

(9-12) HAM, MANGO & RED ONION MIX
Heat 1 teaspoon of the oil in a heavy-bottomed skillet over low heat. Add 1 teaspoon of the onion and cook 10 minutes until completely soft. Transfer to a blender and add 1¾ ounces of the ham, 2 tablespoons of the mango and 3 tablespoons water. Pulse 15 seconds, adding extra water 1 teaspoon at a time, until the mixture forms a lumpy puree. Serve warm.

This Creole mayonnaise is very quick to make and will jazz up any type of sandwich. Here I've put it with slices of steak—but you can also use leftover roast beef. My mother grew up in New Orleans, so she loves the Creole flavors in this.

Steak Sandwich with Creole Mayonnaise

SERVES: 2 adults, 1 child and 1 baby
PREPARATION TIME: 15 minutes
COOKING TIME: 8 minutes
STORAGE: Refrigerate the cooked steak up to 1 day. Refrigerate the mayonnaise up to 2 weeks.

. . . .

3 sirloin steaks
1 tablespoon extra virgin olive oil
3 wholewheat rolls, halved horizontally
2 tomatoes, thinly sliced
6 Chinese cabbage leaves
¼ tsp fine sea salt

FOR THE CREOLE MAYONNAISE
½ cup mayonnaise
1 garlic clove, crushed
½ teaspoon Dijon mustard
¼ teaspoon hot pepper sauce
¾ teaspoon paprika
¼ tablespoon fresh oregano or
    ¼ teaspoon dried oregano
½ teaspoon finely chopped thyme
    leaves or a large pinch of dried
    thyme

1 To make the mayonnaise, put all of the ingredients in a small bowl and mix thoroughly. Heat the oil in a skillet over medium heat. Season the steaks lightly with the salt and cook 2 to 4 minutes on each side until they are cooked to your liking. Slice each steak into strips. Let cool, if you like.

2 Spread the mayonnaise generously over the roll halves. Serve the beef warm or cold in the rolls, topped with the tomatoes and Chinese cabbage leaves.

(6-9) STEAK PUREE
Put 1¾ ounces of the steak and 1 teaspoon of the oil in a skillet and cook 10 minutes until the steak is browned and completely cooked through. Transfer to a blender and add 3 tablespoons water. Blend 30 seconds, adding extra water 1 teaspoon at a time, until smooth. Serve warm.

(9-12) STEAK WITH CHINESE CABBAGE
Put 1¾ ounces of the steak and 1 teaspoon of the oil in a skillet and cook 10 minutes until the steak is browned and completely cooked through. Transfer to a blender and add 1 Chinese cabbage leaf and 3 tablespoons water. Pulse 15 seconds, adding extra water 1 teaspoon at a time, until the mixture forms a lumpy puree. Serve warm.

My sister Lauren said this is freakishly tasty and quick—and blew her mind. The Chinese flavors paired with nutty spelt or wholewheat pasta is a delightful surprise. If you have leftovers, the stir-fry is even tastier the next day over rice.

Chinese Five-Spice Pasta

SERVES: 2 adults, 1 child and 1 baby
PREPARATION TIME: 10 minutes
COOKING TIME: 10 minutes
STORAGE: Refrigerate up to 1 day.

. . . .

2 tablespoons extra virgin olive oil
14 ounces ground beef
10½ ounces broccoli, chopped
2 tablespoons tamari soy sauce or
　shoyu soy sauce
1 teaspoon Chinese five-spice
10½ ounces wholegrain spelt conchiglie
　or wholewheat conchiglie
3 scallions, green part only,
　finely sliced, to serve

1 Heat the oil in a large, heavy-bottomed skillet over medium-high heat. Add the ground beef and broccoli and cook 5 to 10 minutes until the broccoli is cooked but still crunchy and the ground beef has browned and cooked through. (6-9) (9-12) Add the tamari, Chinese five-spice and 4 tablespoons water and mix well.

2 Meanwhile, cook the pasta in plenty of boiling water, according to the package directions. Drain well, add to the beef and broccoli mixture and mix well. Serve hot, sprinkled with scallions.

(6-9)

BEEF & BROCCOLI PUREE
Heat a skillet over medium-low heat until hot. Add 4 tablespoons each of the cooked beef and cooked broccoli and 1 tablespoon water. Cook, stirring occasionally, 10 minutes until the beef is completely cooked through and the broccoli is completely soft. Transfer to a blender and add 3 tablespoons water. Blend 30 seconds, adding extra water 1 teaspoon at a time, until smooth. Serve warm.

(9-12)

BEEF, BROCCOLI & SCALLION
Heat a skillet over medium-low heat until hot. Add 4 tablespoons each of the cooked beef and cooked broccoli, 1 teaspoon of the scallion and 1 tablespoon water. Cook, stirring occasionally, 10 minutes until the beef is completely cooked through and the broccoli is completely soft. Transfer to a blender and add 3 tablespoons water. Pulse 15 seconds, adding extra water 1 teaspoon at a time, until the mixture forms a lumpy puree. Serve warm.

Pretty and packed with flavor, this dish uses corn pasta because it's gluten-free and works for older babies. You can use any type of gluten-free pasta such as rice, millet or quinoa. My kids like these vegetables, but I also make it with peas, broccoli and asparagus.

Shrimp & Tricolor Vegetable Pasta

SERVES: 2 adults, 1 child and 1 baby
PREPARATION TIME: 15 minutes
COOKING TIME: 12 minutes
STORAGE: Refrigerate up to 1 day.

....

1 carrot, halved lengthwise and sliced
7 ounces green beans, trimmed
   and halved
7 ounces artichoke hearts in water or oil,
   drained, bottled or tinned, chopped
3 tablespoons extra virgin olive oil
2 garlic cloves, crushed
½ cup white wine or water
1 tablespoon lemon juice
3 tablespoons butter
1 teaspoon fine sea salt
10½ ounces cooked jumbo shrimp
10½ ounces corn pasta or gluten-free
   pasta, any shape

1 Put the carrot in a steamer and steam, covered, 3 minutes. Add the green beans and steam, covered, 3 minutes longer until they are both cooked but still slightly crunchy. **(6-9)** **(9-12)** Transfer to a bowl, add the artichokes and mix well. Heat 2 tablespoons of the oil in a large, heavy-bottomed skillet over medium heat. Add the garlic and cook 1 minute, then pour in the wine and add the lemon juice, butter and salt. Bring to a boil over high heat, then reduce the heat to medium and cook 2 minutes. Add the shrimp and cook 2 minutes longer until the shrimp are hot.

2 Meanwhile, cook the pasta in plenty of boiling water, according to the package directions. Drain well and add to the vegetable mixture, then add the remaining oil and mix. Add the pasta and vegetables to the shrimp mixture and stir well. Serve warm.

(6-9) **GREEN BEAN, CARROT & ARTICHOKE PUREE**
Leave 3 tablespoons of the green beans and carrots in the steamer and steam, covered, 20 minutes longer until completely soft. Transfer to a blender and add 2 tablespoons of the artichokes and 3 tablespoons water. Blend 30 seconds, adding extra water 1 teaspoon at a time, until smooth. Mix in 1 teaspoon of the oil and serve warm.

(9-12) **VEGETABLES WITH CORN PASTA**
Leave 2 tablespoons of the green beans and carrots in the steamer and steam, covered, 20 minutes longer until completely soft. Mix with 1 tablespoon of the artichokes and 2 tablespoons of chopped, cooked pasta (without the vegetable mixture and oil). Transfer to a blender and add 3 tablespoons water. Pulse 15 seconds, adding extra water 1 teaspoon at a time, until the mixture forms a lumpy puree. Mix in 1 teaspoon of the oil and serve warm.

My children love sardines, but if yours don't, this is an excellent way to serve them because the fishy taste isn't too strong. These little fish are packed with omega-3 essential fats, so they're great for kids. Jessie loves these fish cakes so much that she asks for them every week and is learning to make them.

Sardine Fish Cakes

MAKES: 10
PREPARATION TIME: 20 minutes
COOKING TIME: 30 minutes
STORAGE: Refrigerate up to 1 day.

· ·

14 ounces potatoes, diced
2 extra-large eggs
6¼ ounces canned sardines in oil or water, drained
1 small onion, finely chopped
1 tablespoon Dijon mustard
3 tablespoons chopped parsley leaves
2 teaspoons finely grated lemon zest
a large pinch of cayenne pepper
½ teaspoon fine sea salt
¾ cup dried wholewheat breadcrumbs
1 tablespoon extra virgin olive oil, plus extra for frying if needed
lemon wedges, to serve
salad, to serve

1 Put the potatoes in a steamer and steam, covered, 10 minutes or until soft. Transfer to a large bowl and mash coarsely.

2 In a bowl, beat the eggs together with a whisk. (6-9) (9-12) In another bowl, mash the sardines with a fork. Add the eggs, onion, mustard, parsley, lemon zest, cayenne pepper, salt and breadcrumbs and mix well. Add to the mashed potatoes and mix until well combined. Using your hands, divide the mixture into 10 equal balls and shape each one into a fish cake.

3 Heat the oil in a large, heavy-bottomed skillet over medium-low heat. Working in batches, carefully add the fish cakes to the skillet and cook 3 minutes on each side until browned and heated through. Repeat with the remaining fish cakes, adding more oil to the skillet as needed. Serve warm with lemon wedges and salad.

6-9 SARDINE PUREE
Put 4 sardines and 3 tablespoons water in a blender. Blend 30 seconds, adding extra water 1 teaspoon at a time, until smooth. Serve warm.

9-12 SARDINE, ONION & PARSLEY MIX
Heat 1 teaspoon of the oil in a heavy-bottomed skillet over low heat. Add 1 teaspoon of the onion and cook 10 minutes until completely soft. Transfer to a blender and add 4 sardines, 1 teaspoon of the parsley and 3 tablespoons water. Pulse 15 seconds, adding extra water 1 teaspoon at a time, until the mixture forms a lumpy puree. Serve warm.

This is easy, delicious and very versatile. For a vegetarian version, you can make it without the mackerel and simply top the cooked vegetables with a dollop of bean dip (see page 68). You can change the vegetables, too. I like potato as the base, but you might like sweet potato, spinach or fava beans.

Mackerel on Veg

SERVES: 2 adults, 1 child and 1 baby
PREPARATION TIME: 20 minutes
COOKING TIME: 20 minutes
STORAGE: Refrigerate up to 1 day.

. . . .

10½ ounces potatoes, diced
7 ounces squash, seeded and cut into
    chunks, or pumpkin, peeled, seeded
    and cut into chunks
1 small carrot, chopped
1 small leek, chopped
10 garlic cloves
2½ ounces broccoli, cut into small
    florets
2½ ounces green beans, trimmed
    and halved
14 ounces mackerel fillets
extra virgin olive oil, to serve

1 (6-9) (9-12) Put the potatoes, squash, carrot, leek and garlic in a steamer and steam, covered, 12 to 15 minutes. Add the broccoli and green beans, put the mackerel on top of the vegetables and steam, covered, 5 minutes longer until the vegetables are tender and the mackerel is cooked through. Serve warm with extra virgin olive oil.

(6-9) MACKEREL & VEGETABLE PUREE
Put 2 squash pieces in a steamer and steam, covered, 10 minutes. Add 1 tablespoon of the carrot and steam, covered, 10 minutes longer. Add 3 pieces each of the broccoli and green beans and steam, covered, 10 minutes longer until the vegetables are completely soft. Remove the skin and any bones from 1¾ ounces of the steamed mackerel. Transfer to a blender and add the steamed vegetables and 3 tablespoons water. Blend 30 seconds, adding extra water 1 teaspoon at a time, until smooth. Mix in 1 teaspoon of the oil and serve warm.

(9-12) MACKEREL & VEGETABLE MEDLEY
Put 2 squash pieces in a steamer and steam, covered, 10 minutes. Add 1 tablespoon of the carrot and steam, covered, 10 minutes longer. Add 1 of the garlic cloves, 2 leek pieces and 3 pieces each of the broccoli and green beans and steam, covered, 10 minutes longer until the vegetables are completely soft. Remove the skin and any bones from 1¾ ounces of the steamed mackerel, then transfer to a bowl and mash with a fork. Transfer to a blender and add the steamed vegetables and 3 tablespoons water. Pulse 15 seconds, adding extra water 1 teaspoon at a time, until the mixture forms a lumpy puree. Mix in 1 teaspoon of the oil and serve warm with the mashed mackerel.

My mom sometimes makes this cauliflower for us the day we fly home to see her and my dad over the Christmas vacation. It's a light snack to tide us over until dinner after the long flight. I've added salmon for a great lunch and if you serve it with a little rice, pasta or bread, you have a complete meal.

Baked Salmon, Cauli & Capers

SERVES: 2 adults, 1 child and 1 baby
PREPARATION TIME: 20 minutes, plus at least 7 hours soaking and 40 minutes cooking the brown rice
COOKING TIME: 20 minutes
STORAGE: Refrigerate up to 1 day.

....

6 tablespoons extra virgin olive oil
3 salmon steaks
1 cauliflower, sliced into circles
¼ teaspoon fine sea salt
1 red onion, thinly sliced into rings
4 tablespoons small capers in salt or brine, drained and rinsed
3 garlic cloves, finely chopped
4 tablespoons chopped parsley leaves
freshly ground black pepper
1 recipe quantity cooked brown rice (see page 23), to serve

1 (6-9) (9-12) Preheat the oven to 400°F and grease a large baking sheet with 2 tablespoons of the oil. Arrange the salmon and cauliflower in a single layer on the bottom of the baking sheet and drizzle the remaining oil over the top. Sprinkle with the salt and season with pepper. Top each salmon steak with ⅓ of the onion rings.

2 Bake 15 to 20 minutes until the cauliflower is tender and browned around the edges and the salmon is opaque and cooked through. Serve hot sprinkled with the capers, garlic and parsley, and with the cooked brown rice.

(6-9) **SALMON & CAULIFLOWER PUREE**
Remove the skin and any bones from 1¾ ounces of the salmon. Transfer to a greased baking dish, add 6 cauliflower pieces and bake as above 20 minutes until the salmon is opaque and completely cooked through and the cauliflower is completely soft. Transfer to a blender and add 3 tablespoons water. Blend 30 seconds, adding extra water 1 teaspoon at a time, until smooth. Serve warm.

(9-12) **BAKED SALMON & VEGETABLES**
Remove the skin and any bones from 1¾ ounces of the salmon. Transfer to a greased baking dish, add 6 cauliflower pieces and 1 onion ring and bake as above 20 minutes until the salmon is opaque and completely cooked through and the vegetables are completely soft. Transfer to a blender and add 3 tablespoons water. Pulse 15 seconds, adding extra water 1 teaspoon at a time, until the mixture forms a lumpy puree. Serve warm.

My sister Lauren thinks this is a phenomenal recipe. I know she loves the flavors—and I love the fabulous ingredients such as fava beans, sprouts, beets and toasted seeds. It's a beautiful salad—and filling enough to be a satisfying meal.

Dreamy Salad with Squash

SERVES: 2 adults, 1 child and 1 baby
PREPARATION TIME: 30 minutes
COOKING TIME: 25 minutes
STORAGE: Use the same day.

....

1 butternut squash, seeded and cut into bite-size pieces
6 tablespoons extra virgin olive oil
½ teaspoon fine sea salt
3½ ounces shelled fava beans
3 tablespoons pumpkin seeds
3 tablespoons sunflower seeds
1 tablespoon tamari soy sauce or shoyu soy sauce
3½ ounces feta cheese, cut into bite-size pieces
¼ lettuce, such as romaine, washed and chopped
1 avocado, peeled, pitted and cut into bite-size pieces
1 beet, grated
1 tablespoon balsamic vinegar
1¾ ounces sprouts, such as alfalfa, broccoli or mung (optional)
freshly ground black pepper

1 Preheat the broiler to medium. Put the squash in a baking dish with 2 tablespoons of the oil and toss well. Broil 20 minutes until tender. (6-9) (9-12) Remove from the broiler, sprinkle the salt over the top and season with pepper. Meanwhile, put the the fava beans in a steamer and steam, covered, 3 to 4 minutes until they are cooked but still retain a slight bite.

2 Heat a large skillet over medium-low heat. Mix together the seeds and tamari in a small bowl. Add the seed mix to the skillet and cook, stirring with a wooden spoon, 3 to 5 minutes until the skillet is dry and the seeds are lightly browned.

3 Put the broiled squash, steamed fava beans, feta, lettuce, avocado, beet, toasted seeds, balsamic vinegar, sprouts, if using, and the remaining oil in a large bowl. Toss well and serve.

(6-9) **SQUASH, FAVA BEAN & AVOCADO PUREE**
Put 2 tablespoons of the broiled squash, 1 tablespoon of the steamed fava beans, 2 tablespoons of the avocado and 3 tablespoons water in a blender. Blend 30 seconds, adding extra water 1 teaspoon at a time, until smooth. Serve warm.

(9-12) **SQUASH, FAVA BEAN & AVOCADO WITH BEET & SPROUTS**
Put 2 tablespoons of the broiled squash, 1 tablespoon each of the steamed fava beans, avocado, beet and sprouts, if using, and 3 tablespoons water in a blender. Pulse 15 seconds, adding extra water 1 teaspoon at a time, until the mixture forms a lumpy puree. Serve warm.

I first tried spelt salad in Tuscany. Friends nearby invited us to a picnic on a roasting hot summer day near a freezing mountain stream. After we had all cooled off, we shared the food we had brought. Our friend Susanna offered spelt salad for us to try, which is a classic dish in the region.

Tuscan Spelt Salad

SERVES: 2 adults, 1 child and 1 baby
PREPARATION TIME: 20 minutes, plus at least 7 hours soaking (optional)
COOKING TIME: 35-45 minutes
STORAGE: Refrigerate up to 3 days.

....

¾ cup wholegrain spelt grain
¾ tablespoon plain yogurt or kefir, for soaking (optional)
1 teaspoon fine sea salt
4 tablespoons extra virgin olive oil
2 tablespoons white wine vinegar
9 ounces mozzarella cheese, diced
1 large tomato, chopped
1 zucchini, quartered lengthwise and sliced
1 fennel bulb, chopped
1 small red onion, finely chopped
1 small garlic clove, finely chopped
3 tablespoons chopped parsley leaves
2 tablespoons finely chopped mint leaves

1 If soaking the spelt grain, put the spelt grain and yogurt in a large saucepan and cover generously with warm water. Let soak, covered, 7 hours or overnight at room temperature. Drain and rinse the grains, then return to the pan and add 1½ cups water.

2 Bring to a boil over high heat. Turn the heat down to low and simmer, covered, 30 to 35 minutes, stirring occasionally, until the grains are tender but not mushy. Drain and transfer to a large bowl.

(If cooking unsoaked spelt grain, put the spelt grain and 2 cups water in a large saucepan. Bring to a boil over high heat. Turn the heat down to low and simmer, covered, 45 minutes, stirring occasionally, until the grains are tender but not mushy. Drain and transfer to a large bowl.)

3 (6-9) (9-12) Add the salt, oil and white wine vinegar and mix well. Let cool slightly, then add all of the remaining ingredients and mix well. Serve either warm or cold.

(6-9)

ZUCCHINI PUREE
Put ½ of the sliced zucchini in a steamer and steam, covered, 10 minutes until completely soft. Transfer to a blender and add 2 tablespoons water. Blend 30 seconds, adding extra water 1 teaspoon at a time, until smooth. Mix in 1 teaspoon of the oil and serve warm.

(9-12)

ZUCCHINI, FENNEL, RED ONION & HERB MIX
Put ½ of the sliced zucchini, 1 tablespoon of the fennel and 1 teaspoon of the onion in a steamer and steam, covered, 10 minutes until completely soft. Transfer to a blender and add a pinch each of the parsley and mint leaves and 2 tablespoons water. Pulse 15 seconds, adding extra water 1 teaspoon at a time, until the mixture forms a lumpy puree. Mix in 1 teaspoon of the oil and serve warm.

I love a well-made mushroom soup. In this one, the flavors are deepened by the dried porcini or shiitake mushrooms and by browning off the mushrooms first. Pureeing the soup halfway produces a great texture, leaving chunks of mushroom, leek and parsley.

Simple Mushroom Soup

SERVES: 2 adults, 1 child and 1 baby
PREPARATION TIME: 30 minutes, plus at least 7 hours soaking and 20 minutes cooking the buckwheat
COOKING TIME: 55 minutes
STORAGE: Refrigerate up to 3 days, or freeze up to 3 months.

....

1 ounce dried porcini or shiitake mushrooms
4 tablespoons extra virgin olive oil, plus extra to serve
1 leek, halved lengthwise and sliced
1 pound button mushrooms, sliced
1 recipe quantity cooked buckwheat (see page 22)
2 teaspoons finely chopped thyme leaves
2½ teaspoons fine sea salt
4 tablespoons chopped parsley leaves
wholegrain bread, to serve

1 Soak the porcini mushrooms in 1 cup boiling water 10 minutes until softened. Drain the mushrooms, squeeze out any excess water and chop.

2 (6-9) (9-12) Heat the oil in a large, heavy-bottomed skillet over medium-high heat. Add the leek and cook, stirring occasionally, 10 minutes until soft. Add the porcini and button mushrooms and cook 10 minutes until the mushrooms are beginning to brown.

3 Pour 3 cups boiling water into a large, heavy-bottomed saucepan and stir in the mushroom and leek mixture, cooked buckwheat, thyme and salt. Bring to a boil over high heat, then turn the heat down to low and simmer, covered, 35 minutes.

4 Add the parsley, then transfer ½ of the soup to a blender and blend until smooth. Return the blended soup to the pan, reheating if necessary. Serve hot with extra oil and wholegrain bread.

 BUCKWHEAT PUREE
Put 4 tablespoons of the cooked buckwheat and generous ½ cup water in a saucepan and simmer, covered, over low heat 20 minutes until completely soft. Transfer to a blender and add 2 tablespoons water. Blend 30 seconds, adding extra water 1 teaspoon at a time, until smooth. Mix in 1 teaspoon of the oil and serve warm.

(9-12) **BUCKWHEAT & LEEK MIX**
Put 4 tablespoons of the cooked buckwheat and generous ½ cup water in a saucepan and simmer, covered, over low heat 20 minutes until completely soft. Transfer to a blender and add 2 tablespoons of the cooked leek and 2 tablespoons water. Pulse 15 seconds, adding extra water 1 teaspoon at a time, until the mixture forms a lumpy puree. Mix in 1 teaspoon of the oil and serve warm.

We love hummus, but prefer this dip because of the dreamy creaminess created by the cannellini beans (my brother David's suggestion). When Cassie sees me putting beans in the blender she exclaims, "hummy" with glee. We eat it by the bowlful with toppings and veg.

Bean Dip Feast

SERVES: 2 adults, 1 child and 1 baby
PREPARATION TIME: 20 minutes, plus at least 12 hours soaking and 1 hour 10 minutes cooking the cannellini beans (optional), and at least 12 hours soaking and 2 hours 10 minutes cooking the chickpeas (optional)
COOKING TIME: 5 minutes
STORAGE: Refrigerate the dip up to 3 days.

·····································

heaped ⅓ cup pine nuts
3 tablespoons extra virgin olive oil
3 tablespoons chopped parsley leaves
3 pinches of paprika
2 carrots, cut into circles, to serve
1 cucumber, cut into circles, to serve
1 small yellow bell pepper, halved, seeded, and cut into chunks, to serve
1 endive, leaves separated, to serve
wholewheat pita breads, to serve

FOR THE BEAN DIP
1 recipe quantity cooked dried cannellini beans (see page 23) or 1½ cups drained and rinsed canned cannellini beans
1 recipe quantity cooked dried chickpeas (see page 24) or 1½ cups drained and rinsed canned chickpeas
3 tablespoons lemon juice
6 tablespoons extra virgin olive oil
2 garlic cloves, crushed
2 teaspoons fine sea salt
6 tablespoons tahini

1 Preheat the broiler to medium. Put the pine nuts on a baking sheet and toast under the broiler 3 to 5 minutes until beginning to brown.

2 (6-9) (9-12) To make the bean dip, put the cooked cannellini beans and cooked chickpeas in a food processor or blender. (Add the kombu, if used during cooking.) Add the lemon juice, oil, garlic, salt and scant 1 cup water and blend 1 minute until smooth, then add the tahini and mix well.

3 Spoon 6 tablespoons of the dip into three bowls and drizzle each with 1 tablespoon of the oil. Sprinkle 1 tablespoon of the toasted pine nuts, 1 tablespoon of the parsley and a pinch of paprika over the top of each bowl. Serve the dip with the carrots, cucumber, bell pepper, endive leaves and wholewheat pita breads.

(6-9) CANNELLINI & CHICKPEA PUREE
Put 2 tablespoons each of the cooked cannellini beans and cooked chickpeas and 2 tablespoons water in a blender. Blend 30 seconds, adding extra water 1 teaspoon at a time, until smooth. Mix in 1 teaspoon of the oil and serve warm.

(9-12) CANNELLINI & CHICKPEAS WITH CUCUMBER
Put 2 tablespoons each of the cooked cannellini beans and cooked chickpeas, 4 cucumber pieces and 1 tablespoon water in a blender. Pulse 15 seconds, adding extra water 1 teaspoon at a time, until the mixture forms a lumpy puree. Mix in 1 teaspoon of the oil and serve warm.

Eggs are the perfect protein and if you mix them with a load of vegetables and some rice, you get a wonderfully simple meal that is quick but nourishing.

Rainbow Veg & Rice Omelet

SERVES: 2 adults, 1 child and 1 baby
PREPARATION TIME: 10 minutes, plus at least 7 hours soaking and 40 minutes cooking the brown rice
COOKING TIME: 16 minutes
STORAGE: Refrigerate up to 1 day.

....

6 extra-large eggs
½ teaspoon fine sea salt
¼ teaspoon hot pepper sauce
3 tablespoons extra virgin olive oil
3½ ounces asparagus, woody ends removed and stalks chopped
1 small red bell pepper, halved, seeded and diced
3½ ounces mushrooms, sliced
1 small onion, finely chopped
1 small zucchini, grated
1 carrot, grated
2 garlic cloves, finely chopped
½ recipe quantity cooked brown rice (see page 23)

1 In a bowl, lightly beat the eggs together with a whisk. Add the salt and hot pepper sauce and whisk. Heat 2 tablespoons of the oil in a large, heavy-bottomed skillet over medium-high heat. (9-12) Add the asparagus, bell pepper, mushrooms and onion and cook, stirring occasionally, 5 minutes. (6-9) Add the zucchini, carrot, garlic and cooked brown rice, and cook 3 minutes longer until any juice from the vegetables has evaporated, the rice has warmed through and the vegetables are beginning to brown.

2 Transfer the vegetable and rice mixture to a bowl. Reduce the heat to medium and add the remaining oil to the skillet, tilting the skillet to evenly coat the bottom. Add the eggs and cook 4 to 5 minutes until the eggs are just beginning to set, then spoon the rice and vegetable mixture evenly over the top. Cover partially with a lid and cook 3 minutes longer until the omelet is just cooked through and browned and crisp on the bottom. Serve hot.

(6-9) BROWN RICE, ZUCCHINI & CARROT PUREE
Put 4 tablespoons of the cooked brown rice, 1 tablespoon of the zucchini, 1 tablespoon of the carrot and generous ½ cup boiling water in a saucepan and simmer, covered, over low heat 20 minutes until completely soft. Transfer to a blender and blend 30 seconds, adding water 1 teaspoon at a time, until smooth. Mix in 1 teaspoon of the oil and serve warm.

(9-12) BROWN RICE WITH ASPARAGUS, ZUCCHINI & CARROT
Put 4 tablespoons of the cooked brown rice and generous ½ cup boiling water in a saucepan and simmer, covered, over low heat 10 minutes. Add 3 asparagus pieces and simmer 10 minutes longer until completely soft. Remove from the heat and mix in 1 tablespoon each of the zucchini and carrot. Transfer to a blender and pulse 15 seconds, adding water 1 teaspoon at a time, until the mixture forms a lumpy puree. Mix in 1 teaspoon of the oil and serve warm.

To my horror, my friend Kate told me that she doesn't like quinoa. What's not to like? I met the challenge with a plea for her to make these tomatoes at home. She did, said it's a great recipe and is now a convert.

Quinoa-Stuffed Tomatoes

SERVES: 2 adults, 1 child and 1 baby
PREPARATION TIME: 20 minutes, plus at least 7 hours soaking and 20 minutes cooking the quinoa
COOKING TIME: 35 minutes
STORAGE: Refrigerate up to 3 days.

....

⅓ cup pine nuts
2 tablespoons extra virgin olive oil, plus extra for greasing
1 leek, quartered lengthwise and sliced
½ recipe quantity cooked quinoa (see page 22)
2¾ ounces Parmesan cheese, grated
1 garlic clove, crushed
½ teaspoon fine sea salt
3 large tomatoes
salad, to serve

1 Preheat the broiler to medium. Put the pine nuts on a baking sheet and toast under the broiler 3 minutes until lightly browned.

2 Preheat the oven to 315°F and grease a large baking dish with oil. (6-9) (9-12) Heat the oil in a heavy-bottomed saucepan over medium heat. Add the leek and cook, stirring occasionally, 10 minutes until soft.

3 Mix the toasted pine nuts, cooked leek, cooked quinoa, Parmesan, garlic and salt in a small bowl. Cut the tomatoes in half horizontally, then scoop out and discard the flesh and seeds. Spoon the quinoa mixture into each tomato half until filled to the top. Put the stuffed tomatoes in the baking dish and bake 20 minutes until the cheese has melted and is beginning to brown. Serve hot with salad.

(6-9)

QUINOA PUREE
Put 4 tablespoons of the cooked quinoa and generous ½ cup boiling water in a saucepan and simmer, covered, over low heat 20 minutes until completely soft. Transfer to a blender and add 2 tablespoons water. Blend 30 seconds, adding extra water 1 teaspoon at a time, until smooth. Mix in 1 teaspoon of the oil and serve warm.

(9-12)

QUINOA WITH LEEKS
Put 4 tablespoons of the cooked quinoa and generous ½ cup boiling water in a saucepan and simmer, covered, over low heat 20 minutes until completely soft. Transfer to a blender and add 1 tablespoon of the cooked leeks and 2 tablespoons water. Pulse 15 seconds, adding extra water 1 teaspoon at a time, until the mixture forms a lumpy puree. Mix in 1 teaspoon of the oil and serve warm.

Wild rice is a great food that many people either don't know about or forget about. It has a wonderfully chewy texture and a slight nutty flavour. You can also use other types of rice or pasta when you feel like a change.

Wild Rice Pancakes

MAKES: 12
PREPARATION TIME: 15 minutes, plus at least 7 hours soaking and 40 minutes cooking the wild rice
COOKING TIME: 18 minutes
STORAGE: Refrigerate up to 3 days.

....

2 extra-large eggs
½ cup wholegrain spelt flour or wholewheat flour
1 recipe quantity cooked wild rice (see page 23)
2 tablespoons plain yogurt
3½ ounces fresh or defrosted, frozen baby spinach leaves, finely chopped
3½ ounces feta cheese, diced
¾ teaspoon fine sea salt
½ teaspoon cayenne pepper
1 tablespoon extra virgin olive oil, plus extra for frying if needed
salad, to serve

1 Put the eggs and 2 tablespoons water in a large mixing bowl and lightly beat together with a whisk. (6-9) (9-12) Whisk in the flour, then add the cooked wild rice, yogurt, spinach, feta, salt and cayenne pepper and mix well.

2 Heat the oil in a large, heavy-bottomed skillet over medium heat. Working in batches, pour 2 tablespoons of the batter into the skillet to make a pancake and repeat, spacing the pancakes slightly apart. Cook 3 minutes on each side or until lightly browned. Repeat with the remaining batter, adding more oil to the skillet as needed. Serve warm with salad.

(6-9) WILD RICE PUREE
Put 4 tablespoons of the cooked wild rice and scant ⅔ cup boiling water in a saucepan and simmer, covered, over low heat 20 minutes until completely soft. Transfer the rice to a blender and add 2 tablespoons water. Blend 30 seconds, adding extra water 1 teaspoon at a time, until smooth. Mix in 1 teaspoon of the oil and serve warm.

(9-12) WILD RICE WITH YOGURT
Put 4 tablespoons of the cooked wild rice and scant ⅔ cup boiling water in a saucepan and simmer, covered, over low heat 20 minutes until completely soft. Transfer the rice to a blender and add 2 tablespoons of the yogurt and 1 tablespoon water. Pulse 15 seconds, adding extra water 1 teaspoon at a time, until the mixture forms a lumpy puree. Mix in 1 teaspoon of the oil and serve warm.

Fried Root Rosti
with Poached Eggs

MAKES: 6
PREPARATION TIME: 20 minutes, plus 7 hours soaking and 40 minutes cooking the brown rice
COOKING TIME: 25 minutes
STORAGE: Refrigerate the uncooked rosti mixture up to 1 day.

....

7 extra-large eggs
1 large sweet potato, grated
1 small rutabaga or 2 parsnips, peeled and grated
½ recipe quantity cooked brown rice (see page 23)
4 tablespoons wholegrain spelt flour or wholewheat flour
1 tablespoon wholegrain mustard
1 teaspoon fine sea salt
2 tablespoons extra virgin olive oil, plus extra for frying if needed
1 tablespoon white wine vinegar or grape vinegar
freshly ground black pepper
salad, to serve

1 Preheat the oven to 200°F. In a large mixing bowl, lightly beat 1 of the eggs with a whisk. (6-9) (9-12) Add the sweet potato, rutabaga, cooked brown rice, flour, mustard and salt and mix well.

2 Heat the oil in a large, heavy-bottomed skillet over medium-high heat. Working in batches, scoop 4 tablespoons of the mixture into your hand and shape it into a rosti. Using the back of a metal spoon, flatten the top and and smooth the sides. Flip your hand over so the rosti lands in the skillet and flatten the top with a spatula. Cook 4 to 5 minutes on each side until golden brown. Repeat with the remaining mixture, adding more oil to the skillet as needed. Keep the rostis warm in the oven while you poach the eggs.

3 Bring a large saucepan of water to a boil, then turn the heat down to low. Add the vinegar, then crack 1 egg into the gently simmering water. Repeat with the remaining 5 eggs and simmer 3 minutes. Remove the eggs from the pan, using a slotted spoon, and drain on a plate lined with paper towels. Top each rosti with a poached egg, season with pepper and serve warm with salad.

(6-9) SWEET POTATO, RUTABAGA & RICE PUREE

Put 1 tablespoon each of the sweet potato and rutabaga, 4 tablespoons of the cooked brown rice, 1 teaspoon of the oil and generous ½ cup water in a heavy-bottomed skillet. Cook, covered, over low heat 20 minutes until completely soft. Transfer to a blender and add 3 tablespoons water. Blend 30 seconds, adding extra water 1 teaspoon at a time, until smooth. Serve warm.

(9-12) RUTABAGA & BROWN RICE WITH SWEET POTATO

Put 2 tablespoons of the rutabaga, 4 tablespoons of the cooked brown rice, 1 teaspoon of the oil and generous ½ cup water in a heavy-bottomed skillet. Cook, covered, over low heat 20 minutes until completely soft. Transfer to a blender and add 2 tablespoons of the sweet potato and 3 tablespoons water. Pulse 15 seconds, adding extra water 1 teaspoon at a time, until the mixture forms a lumpy puree. Serve warm.

I offered this lunch recipe to my friend Julia, who made it with some hesitation. However, she came back with rave reviews, remarking on the wonderfully lively flavors of lime juice, cumin and cilantro—and thinks it's a perfect summer dish.

Spiced Red Beans with Corn & Rice

SERVES: 2 adults, 1 child and 1 baby
PREPARATION TIME: 25 minutes, plus at least 12 hours soaking and 1 hour 40 minutes cooking the kidney beans (optional), plus 1 hour standing, plus at least 7 hours soaking and 40 minutes cooking the brown rice
COOKING TIME: 4 minutes
STORAGE: Refrigerate up to 3 days.

....

heaped 1 cup frozen corn kernels
1 recipe quantity cooked dried kidney beans (see page 24) or 2½ cups drained and rinsed canned kidney beans
1 orange bell pepper, seeded and diced
1 small red onion, finely chopped
1 garlic clove, finely chopped
5 tablespoons extra virgin olive oil
4 tablespoons lime juice
1 teaspoon ground cumin
2 teaspoons fine sea salt
1 recipe quantity cooked brown rice (see page 23)
8 tablespoons chopped cilantro leaves

1 Put the corn kernels in a steamer and steam, covered, 3 to 4 minutes until just tender.

2 (6-9) (9-12) Put the cooked kidney beans in a large bowl. (Chop and add the kombu, if used during cooking.) Add the steamed corn kernels, bell pepper, onion, garlic, oil, lime juice, cumin and ½ of the salt and mix well. Cover and let stand at room temperature at least 1 hour.

3 Put the cooked brown rice in a large bowl, add the remaining salt and mix well. Mix the cilantro into the bean mixture and serve over the warm rice.

(6-9) **RED BEAN & BROWN RICE PUREE**
Put 4 tablespoons of the cooked brown rice and generous ½ cup boiling water in a saucepan and simmer, covered, over low heat 20 minutes until completely soft. Transfer to a blender and add 2 tablespoons of the cooked kidney beans and 3 tablespoons water. Blend 30 seconds, adding extra water 1 teaspoon at a time, until smooth. Mix in 1 teaspoon of the oil and serve warm.

(9-12) **SPICED RED BEANS & RICE**
Put 4 tablespoons of the cooked brown rice, ½ teaspoon each of the onion and cilantro and generous ½ cup boiling water in a saucepan and simmer, covered, over low heat 20 minutes until completely soft. Transfer to a blender and add 2 tablespoons of the cooked kidney beans and 3 tablespoons water. Pulse 15 seconds, adding extra water 1 teaspoon at a time, until the mixture forms a lumpy puree. Mix in 1 teaspoon of the oil and serve warm.

This simple yet delicious vegetable pasta makes a great lunch. It's a favorite of Jessie's because she loves artichokes and peas, and anything with lemon—which in this dish lifts and brightens the Parmesan cheese.

Corn Pasta with Artichoke & Peas

SERVES: 2 adults, 1 child and 1 baby
PREPARATION TIME: 20 minutes
COOKING TIME: 12 minutes
STORAGE: Refrigerate up to 3 days.

....

5 tablespoons extra virgin olive oil
1 onion, chopped
3 garlic cloves, finely chopped
1 pound drained, bottled or canned artichoke hearts in water or oil, chopped
1½ cups defrosted, frozen peas or fresh, podded peas
1½ ounces Parmesan cheese, grated
2 tablespoons lemon juice
10½ ounces corn or gluten-free pasta
½ teaspoon fine sea salt

1 (6-9) Heat 2 tablespoons of the oil in a large, heavy-bottomed skillet over medium heat. Add the onion and cook, stirring occasionally, 5 minutes until beginning to brown, then turn the heat up to medium-high. Add the garlic and artichokes and cook, stirring occasionally, 5 minutes longer until lightly browned. Add the peas and cook 2 minutes until heated through. (9-12) Transfer to a large bowl, add the Parmesan, lemon juice and 1 tablespoon of the oil and mix well.

2 Meanwhile, cook the pasta in plenty of boiling water, according to the package directions. Drain well, then mix in the salt and the remaining oil. Add the pasta to the artichoke mixture and mix well. Serve warm.

(6-9)

ARTICHOKE & PEA PUREE
Heat 1 teaspoon of the oil and 3 tablespoons water in a skillet over low heat. Add 3 tablespoons of the peas and cook, covered, 10 minutes until completely soft. Add 9 artichoke pieces and cook 2 to 3 minutes longer until the artichoke has warmed through. Transfer to a blender and add 3 tablespoons water. Blend 30 seconds, adding extra water 1 teaspoon at a time, until smooth. Serve warm.

(9-12)

CORN PASTA, ARTICHOKE & PEA
Put 3 tablespoons of the cooked artichoke and pea mixture, 2 tablespoons of chopped, cooked corn pasta (without the salt or oil) and 3 tablespoons water in a blender. Pulse 15 seconds, adding extra water 1 teaspoon at a time, until the mixture forms a lumpy puree. Mix in 1 teaspoon of the oil and serve warm.

Tofu, when marinated, takes on lots of flavor, so it's great with this fabulous marinade. Toasted sesame oil, which is used here, is a wonderful condiment to keep in your kitchen, and tofu can be added to any stir-fry recipe to provide extra protein.

Marinated Tofu Stir-Fry

SERVES: 2 adults, 1 child and 1 baby
PREPARATION TIME: 25 minutes, plus 30 minutes marinating, plus at least 7 hours soaking and 40 minutes cooking the brown rice
COOKING TIME: 15 minutes
STORAGE: Refrigerate up to 3 days.

....

9 ounces tofu, patted dry and cut into bite-size pieces
2 tablespoons sesame seeds
2 tablespoons toasted sesame oil
9 ounces broccoli, cut into bite-size florets
7 ounces snow peas, trimmed and halved
1½ recipe quantities cooked brown rice (see page 23), to serve

FOR THE MARINADE
2 tablespoons lemon juice
4 teaspoons grated ginger root
2 garlic cloves, crushed
3 tablespoons tamari soy sauce or shoyu soy sauce
2 tablespoons toasted sesame oil

1 (9-18) To make the marinade, put all of the ingredients in a nonreactive bowl and mix well. Add the tofu and stir well, making sure the tofu is covered in the marinade. Cover and let marinate at room temperature 30 minutes.

2 Meanwhile, toast the sesame seeds in a dry skillet over medium heat 1 to 2 minutes, stirring occasionally, until golden.

3 Heat the oil in a wok or large skillet over medium heat. Add the tofu to the wok and reserve any remaining marinade. (6-9) Stir-fry 5 minutes until beginning to brown, then add the broccoli, snow peas, the remaining marinade and ½ cup hot water and stir-fry, stirring, 5 minutes longer until the vegetables are soft. Serve hot over the cooked brown rice, with the toasted sesame seeds sprinkled over the top.

(6-9) SNOW PEA, BROCCOLI & BROWN RICE PUREE
Put 4 tablespoons of the cooked brown rice and generous ½ cup boiling water in a saucepan and simmer, covered, over low heat 10 minutes. Add 6 pieces each of the snow peas and broccoli and simmer, covered, 10 minutes longer until completely soft. Transfer to a blender and add 3 tablespoons water. Blend 30 seconds, adding extra water 1 teaspoon at a time, until smooth. Serve warm.

(9-12) SNOW PEA, BROCCOLI, GARLIC & BROWN RICE
Put 4 tablespoons of the cooked brown rice and generous ½ cup boiling water in a saucepan and simmer, covered, over low heat 10 minutes. Add 6 pieces each of the snow peas and broccoli and a pinch of the garlic and simmer, covered, 10 minutes longer until completely soft. Transfer to a blender and add 3 tablespoons water. Pulse 15 seconds, adding extra water 1 teaspoon at a time, until the mixture forms a lumpy puree. Serve warm.

chapter three
around the table

I find that I need a wide selection of dinners.
There are weekdays when there isn't much time
and I haven't planned ahead; weekends when
I am happy to spend a little more time putting
a meal together; and dinners with friends where
I want to create something very special. Whether
you're feeling like meat, chicken or fish; beans
or lentils; or anything from pasta to rice to more
unusual grains, there are recipes to tempt you.

There are spring delights like Herb-Crusted
Fish, summer favorites such as Open Quesadilla
with Salsa, fall treats like Pancetta-Wrapped
Chicken with Quinoa Salad and winter stews,
such as Slowly Simmered Beef & Onion Stew.
These will all provide you with wonderful meals
for the whole family—whether they are 6-month
olds or 60-year olds!

Pancetta-Wrapped Chicken with Quinoa Salad

SERVES: 2 adults, 1 child and 1 baby
PREPARATION TIME: 45 minutes, plus at least 7 hours soaking and 20 minutes cooking the quinoa
COOKING TIME: 40 minutes
STORAGE: Refrigerate the quinoa salad up to 3 days. Refrigerate the chicken up to 1 day.

1 tablespoon extra virgin olive oil
1 tablespoon finely chopped thyme leaves
½ teaspoon paprika
¼ teaspoon fine sea salt
6 boneless, skinless chicken thighs
12 pancetta slices, sliced as thinly as possible, or 6 prosciutto slices
freshly ground black pepper

FOR THE QUINOA SALAD
scant ½ cup frozen peas or fresh, podded peas
2½ ounces green beans, trimmed and chopped
2½ ounces broccoli, cut into bite-size florets
1 small leek, quartered lengthwise and sliced
1 recipe quantity cooked quinoa (see page 22)
1 teaspoon fine sea salt

FOR THE DRESSING
2 tablespoons toasted sesame oil
2 tablespoons extra virgin olive oil
1 tablespoon red miso
4 tablespoons brown rice vinegar

1 (6-9) (9-18) Preheat the oven to 400°F and grease the bottom of a baking dish with the oil. Mix the thyme, paprika and salt in a small, shallow bowl. Put the chicken thighs in the baking dish, then sprinkle the thyme mixture over the top and season with pepper. Wrap 2 slices of the pancetta (or 1 slice of prosciutto) around each thigh, tucking the ends underneath the thigh to secure them. Bake 35 to 40 minutes until the chicken is cooked through and the pancetta has browned.

2 Meanwhile, make the quinoa salad. Put the vegetables in a steamer and steam, covered, 3 minutes until tender. Put the steamed vegetables, cooked quinoa and salt in a large bowl and mix well.

3 To make the dressing, put all of the ingredients in a small jar. Secure with a lid and shake vigorously until the miso has completely dissolved. Pour the dressing over the salad and mix well. Serve warm with the chicken.

(6-9) **CHICKEN & QUINOA PUREE WITH MIXED VEG PUREE**
Put ½ of 1 chicken thigh, 2 tablespoons of the cooked quinoa and generous ½ cup boiling water in a greased baking dish. Bake as above 20 minutes until the chicken is completely cooked through and the juices run clear, and the quinoa is completely soft. Transfer to a blender and add 4 tablespoons water. Blend 30 seconds, adding extra water 1 teaspoon at a time, until smooth. Leave 3 broccoli pieces, 4 green bean pieces and 1 tablespoon of the peas in the steamer and steam, covered, 7 minutes longer until completely soft. Transfer to a blender and add 2 tablespoons water. Blend 30 seconds, adding extra water 1 teaspoon at a time, until smooth. Serve warm with the chicken and quinoa puree.

(9-12) **CHICKEN & QUINOA WITH MIXED VEG & LEEKS**
Put ½ of 1 chicken thigh, 2 tablespoons of the cooked quinoa and generous ½ cup boiling water in a greased baking dish. Bake as above 20 minutes until the chicken is completely cooked through and the juices run clear, and the quinoa is completely soft. Transfer to a blender and add 4 tablespoons water. Pulse 15 seconds, adding extra water 1 teaspoon at a time, until the mixture forms a lumpy puree. Leave 3 broccoli pieces, 4 green bean pieces and 1 tablespoon each of the peas and leeks in the steamer and steam, covered, 7 minutes longer until completely soft. Transfer to a blender and add 2 tablespoons water. Pulse 15 seconds, adding extra water 1 teaspoon at a time, until the mixture forms a lumpy puree. Serve warm with the chicken and quinoa puree.

Chicken Piccata with Baked Sweet Potato & Apple

SERVES: 2 adults, 1 child and 1 baby
PREPARATION TIME: 40 minutes
COOKING TIME: 30 minutes
STORAGE: Refrigerate up to 1 day.

....

2 sweet potatoes, cut into chunks
4 apples, cored and cut into chunks
2 tablespoons wholegrain spelt flour
    or wholewheat flour
1 teaspoon fine sea salt
3 boneless, skinless chicken breasts,
    or 6 boneless, skinless chicken
    thighs, each sliced horizontally into
    2 flat pieces
2 tablespoons unsalted butter
2 tablespoons extra virgin olive oil,
    plus extra for greasing
6 tablespoons lemon juice
1 small lemon, thinly sliced
1 cup white wine
3 tablespoons capers in salt or brine,
    drained and rinsed
6 tablespoons chopped parsley leaves
freshly ground black pepper
steamed vegetables, to serve

1 Preheat the oven to 425°F and grease a large, shallow baking dish with oil. (6-9) (9-12) Put the sweet potatoes, apples and ⅓ cup water in the baking dish and bake 30 minutes until soft and lightly browned.

2 Meanwhile, mix the flour and salt in a shallow bowl and season with pepper. Dip each chicken piece into the flour to coat well, shake off any excess flour and transfer to a plate. Heat ½ of the butter and oil in a large, heavy-bottomed skillet over medium-high heat. Working in batches to avoid overcrowding the skillet, add the chicken and cook 2 to 3 minutes on each side until the chicken is golden brown and cooked through. Remove from the skillet and repeat with the remaining chicken, adding the remaining butter and oil to the skillet as needed. Put the cooked chicken to one side. Remove the skillet from the heat and let cool slightly.

3 Add the lemon juice, lemon slices, wine, capers and parsley to the skillet, then bring to a boil over high heat. Turn the heat down to low and simmer, covered, 10 minutes. Return the chicken to the skillet and cook 2 to 3 minutes until warmed through. Serve warm with the sauce poured over and with the baked sweet potatoes and apples and steamed vegetables.

(6-9) BAKED CHICKEN, SWEET POTATO & APPLE PUREE
Put 1¾ ounces of the chicken, 4 sweet potato chunks, 4 apple chunks and 2 tablespoons water in a baking dish and bake as above 20 minutes until the chicken is completely cooked through and the juices run clear, and the sweet potato and apple are completely soft. Transfer to a blender and add 3 tablespoons water. Blend 30 seconds, adding extra water 1 teaspoon at a time, until smooth. Serve warm.

 BAKED HERBED CHICKEN, SWEET POTATO & APPLE
Put 1¾ ounces of the chicken, 2 sweet potato chunks, 4 apple chunks and 2 tablespoons water in a baking dish and bake as above 20 minutes until the chicken is completely cooked through and the juices run clear, and the sweet potato and apple are completely soft. Transfer to a blender and add 1 teaspoon of the parsley and 3 tablespoons water. Pulse 15 seconds, adding extra water 1 teaspoon at a time, until the mixture forms a lumpy puree. Serve warm.

This is my dad's favorite chicken dish—without the broccoli! He adores how the spicy ingredients are contrasted by a hint of sweetness. The totally gorgeous baby is Niamh Harrison-Murray, the daughter of my friends Nathalie and Diarmid. She is pictured here having some of her first purees.

Edward's Ginger Chicken

SERVES: 2 adults, 1 child and 1 baby
PREPARATION TIME: 30 minutes, plus at least 7 hours soaking and 35 minutes cooking the brown basmati rice
COOKING TIME: 50 minutes
STORAGE: Refrigerate the chicken and sauce up to 1 day. Refrigerate the basmati rice up to 3 days.

....

½ cup extra virgin olive oil
3 boneless, skinless chicken breasts or 6 boneless, skinless chicken thighs
7 scallions, finely sliced
2½ tablespoons finely chopped ginger root
1½ teaspoons chili powder
generous 2 cups chicken stock
1 teaspoon black peppercorns
1 tablespoon cane sugar
1 tablespoon tamari soy sauce or shoyu soy sauce
1 tablespoon cornstarch, ground arrowroot or crushed kuzu
1 recipe quantity cooked brown basmati rice (see page 23)
1 teaspoon salt
steamed broccoli, cut into bite-size florets, to serve

1 Heat the oil in a large, heavy-bottomed skillet over medium-high heat. Add the chicken and cook 3 to 4 minutes on each side until browned.

2 (6-9) (9-12) Add the scallions, ginger, chili powder, stock, peppercorns, sugar and tamari to the skillet. Bring to a boil over medium-high heat, then turn the heat down to low and simmer, covered, 30 to 35 minutes until the chicken is tender and cooked through.

3 In a small bowl, mix the cornstarch and 1 tablespoon cold water together to make a smooth paste. Remove the chicken from the skillet and stir the cornstarch mixture into the liquid remaining in the skillet. Stir over a medium heat 5 minutes or until the sauce is thick and glossy. Put the cooked brown basmati rice in a large bowl, add the salt and mix well. Serve the chicken with the sauce poured over the top and with the rice and steamed broccoli.

(6-9) CHICKEN, BROCCOLI & BROWN BASMATI RICE PUREE
Put 2 tablespoons of the cooked brown basmati rice, 1¾ ounces of the browned chicken and generous ½ cup boiling water in a saucepan. Bring to a boil over high heat, then turn the heat down to low and simmer, covered, 10 minutes. Add 2 tablespoons of steamed broccoli and simmer, covered, 10 minutes longer until the rice is completely soft and the chicken is completely cooked through. Transfer to a blender and add 3 tablespoons water. Blend 30 seconds, adding extra water 1 teaspoon at a time, until smooth. Serve warm.

(9-12) CHICKEN, VEGGIES & BROWN BASMATI RICE
Put 2 tablespoons of the cooked brown basmati rice, 1¾ ounces of the browned chicken, 1 teaspoon of the scallions and generous ½ cup boiling water in a saucepan. Bring to a boil over high heat, then turn the heat down to low and simmer, covered, 10 minutes. Add 2 tablespoons of steamed broccoli and simmer, covered, 10 minutes longer until the rice is completely soft and the chicken is completely cooked through. Transfer to a blender and add 3 tablespoons water. Pulse 15 seconds, adding extra water 1 teaspoon at a time, until the mixture forms a lumpy puree. Serve warm.

Packed with toasted garlic, this simple and tasty chicken is gorgeous served with celeriac slaw. My friend Julia, in Tuscany, served it to her husband Dayton and a builder who was working at their house—and both men gave it the thumbs up.

Garlic Chicken with Celeriac Slaw

SERVES: 2 adults, 1 child and 1 baby
PREPARATION TIME: 30 minutes
COOKING TIME: 40 minutes
STORAGE: Refrigerate the chicken up to 1 day. Refrigerate the slaw up to 3 days.

....

2 tablespoons unsalted butter, plus extra for greasing and to serve
8 garlic cloves, sliced
3 boneless chicken breasts or 6 boneless chicken thighs
1½ teaspoons balsamic vinegar
cooked corn spaghetti or gluten-free spaghetti, to serve
¼ teaspoon fine sea salt, to serve
2 tablespoons extra virgin olive oil, to serve

FOR THE CELERIAC SLAW
1 celeriac, peeled and grated
1½ tablespoons lemon juice
3 tablespoons mayonnaise
1 teaspoon Dijon mustard
1 teaspoon poppy seeds
3 tablespoons extra virgin olive oil

1 Preheat the oven to 400°F and grease a large baking dish with butter. Heat ½ of the butter in a heavy-bottomed skillet over medium heat. Add the garlic and cook 5 minutes until golden brown, then remove the skillet from the heat. (6-9) (9-12) Put the chicken in the baking dish skin-side up. Make 2 slits in the top of each breast, cutting halfway through the meat, and stuff ⅓ of the garlic into each slit. Evenly sprinkle the balsamic vinegar over the chicken breasts and bake 30 to 35 minutes until the chicken skin is crisp and the juices run clear.

2 Meanwhile, make the celeriac slaw. Put all of the ingredients in a large bowl and mix well.

3 Serve the chicken hot with the celeriac slaw and the cooked corn spaghetti tossed with salt, oil and the remaining butter.

(6-9) CHICKEN & CELERIAC PUREE
Put ½ of 1 chicken breast in a greased baking dish, remove the skin and bake as above 15 to 20 minutes until completely cooked through and the juices run clear. Put 2 tablespoons of the celeriac in a steamer and steam, covered, 10 minutes until completely soft. Transfer to a blender and add the cooked chicken and 3 tablespoons water. Blend 30 seconds, adding extra water 1 teaspoon at at time, until smooth. Mix in 1 teaspoon of the oil and serve warm.

(9-12) CHICKEN, CORN SPAGHETTI & GRATED CELERIAC
Put ½ of 1 chicken breast in a greased baking dish, remove the skin and bake as above 15 to 20 minutes until completely cooked through and the juices run clear. Transfer to a blender and add 2 tablespoons of the celeriac, 2 tablespoons of chopped, cooked corn spaghetti and 3 tablespoons water. Pulse 15 seconds, adding extra water 1 teaspoon at a time, until the mixture forms a lumpy puree. Mix in 1 teaspoon of the oil and serve warm.

Stews are a wonderful way to achieve excellent flavors in a dish without a lot of fuss—just throw it together and cook it on the hob or in the oven while you do other things.

Pork & Orange Stew

SERVES: 2 adults, 1 child and 1 baby
PREPARATION TIME: 40 minutes
COOKING TIME: 1 hour 20 minutes
STORAGE: Refrigerate up to 1 day.

....

3 tablespoons extra virgin olive oil
1 pound boneless pork shoulder,
   cut into large chunks
2 carrots, cut into sticks
1 onion, finely chopped
2 garlic cloves, finely chopped
1 tablespoon cornstarch, ground
   arrowroot or crushed kuzu
6 plum tomatoes, finely chopped
1 tablespoon rice malt syrup or
   cane sugar
1 tablespoon orange zest
generous 1 cup chicken stock
generous 1 cup dry white wine
1 teaspoon fine sea salt
cooked rice noodles, to serve

1 (6-9) (9-12) Heat 2 tablespoons of the oil in a large, heavy-bottomed saucepan over medium-high heat. Working in batches to avoid overcrowding the pan, add the pork and cook, stirring frequently, 6 minutes until well browned on all sides. Remove from the pan, using a slotted spoon, and set aside. Repeat with the remaining pork, adding the remaining oil to the pan as needed.

2 Return the pork to the pan and add the carrots, onion and garlic and cook 8 minutes longer until the vegetables are beginning to brown. In a small bowl, mix the cornstarch and 1 tablespoon cold water together to make a smooth paste. Add the tomatoes, rice malt syrup, orange zest, stock, wine, cornstarch mixture and salt and stir well. Bring to a boil over medium-high heat, then turn the heat down to low and simmer, covered, 1 hour until the pork is tender. Serve hot over cooked rice noodles.

(6-9) **PORK, RICE NOODLE & CARROT PUREE**
Heat a heavy-bottomed skillet over medium-low heat until hot. Add 1¾ ounces of the pork, 6 carrot pieces, 1 teaspoon of the oil and 6 tablespoons water. Simmer, covered, 20 minutes until the pork is tender and completely cooked through and the carrots are completely soft. Transfer to a blender and add 2 tablespoons of chopped, cooked rice noodles. Blend 30 seconds, adding water 1 teaspoon at a time, until smooth. Serve warm.

 PORK WITH RICE NOODLES & VEGETABLES
Heat a heavy-bottomed skillet over medium-low heat until hot. Add 1¾ ounces of the pork, 6 carrot pieces, 1 teaspoon of the onion, a pinch of the chopped garlic, 1 teaspoon of the oil and 6 tablespoons water. Simmer, covered, 20 minutes until the pork is tender and completely cooked through and the carrots are completely soft. Transfer to a blender and add 2 tablespoons of chopped, cooked rice noodles. Pulse 15 seconds, adding water 1 teaspoon at a time, until the mixture forms a lumpy puree. Serve warm.

Pork with Capers & Mashed Celeriac

SERVES: 2 adults, 1 child and 1 baby
PREPARATION TIME: 30 minutes
COOKING TIME: 1 hour 35 minutes
STORAGE: Refrigerate the pork
up to 1 day. Refrigerate the mashed
celeriac up to 3 days.

....

2 tablespoons unsalted butter
3 large pork chops or 6 regular
   pork chops
2 onions, finely chopped
3 garlic cloves, finely chopped
1 tablespoon tomato paste
1 ounce drained, bottled or canned
   anchovies in oil, chopped
2 cups chicken stock
2 tablespoons capers in salt or brine,
   drained and rinsed
1½ tablespoons chopped parsley leaves
freshly ground black pepper
steamed vegetables, to serve

FOR THE MASHED CELERIAC
1 celeriac, peeled and cut into chunks
1 pound 2 ounces potatoes, peeled and
   cut into chunks
3½ tablespoons unsalted butter
4 tablespoons extra virgin olive oil
1 tablespoon coarse-grain mustard
½ cup vegetable stock
freshly ground black pepper

1 Heat ½ of the butter in a large, heavy-bottomed skillet over medium-high heat until melted. **(6-9)** **(9-18)** Working in batches, add the pork chops and cook 3 to 5 minutes on each side until browned. Transfer to a plate and season with pepper. Repeat with the remaining pork chops, adding the remaining butter to the skillet as needed.

2 Reduce the heat to medium. Add the onions to the skillet and cook 5 minutes until beginning to brown. Add the garlic, tomato paste, anchovies and stock and mix. Bring to a boil over high heat, stirring with a wooden spoon to lift the dark coating off the bottom of the skillet. Return the pork to the skillet, turn the heat down to low and simmer, covered, 30 minutes. Turn the chops over and simmer, covered, 30 minutes longer. Add the capers and cook 10 minutes until the pork is tender.

3 Meanwhile, make the mashed celeriac. Put the celeriac and potatoes into separate saucepans of cold water and bring to a boil over high heat. Reduce the heat to medium and simmer, covered, cooking the celeriac 15 to 20 minutes and the potatoes 10 to 12 minutes or until both are tender. Drain well and transfer the celeriac and potatoes into one saucepan. Mash the celeriac and potatoes together thoroughly, then mix in the butter, oil and mustard until well combined. Stir in enough stock to make the mash creamy and smooth, then season with pepper to taste. Sprinkle the pork with parsley and serve hot over the mashed celeriac with steamed vegetables.

(6-9) PORK & CELERIAC PUREE
Cut 1¾ ounces of the pork into small pieces. Put the pork, 4 tablespoons of the cooked celeriac (without the other ingredients) and 1 cup boiling water in a saucepan. Simmer, covered, over low heat 20 minutes until the pork is completely cooked through. Transfer to a blender and blend 30 seconds, adding water 1 teaspoon at a time, until smooth. Serve warm.

(9-18) PORK, ANCHOVY & CELERIAC
Cut 1¾ ounces of the pork into small pieces. Put the pork, 4 tablespoons of the cooked celeriac (without the other ingredients), 1 anchovy piece and 1 cup boiling water in a saucepan. Simmer, covered, over low heat 20 minutes until the pork is completely cooked through. Transfer to a blender and pulse 15 seconds, adding water 1 teaspoon at a time, until the mixture forms a lumpy puree. Serve warm.

Lamb Biryani

SERVES: 2 adults, 1 child and 1 baby
PREPARATION TIME: 30 minutes,
plus at least 7 hours soaking, plus
at least 2 hours marinating
COOKING TIME: 1 hour 10 minutes
STORAGE: Refrigerate up to 1 day.

....

heaped 1½ cups brown basmati or long
   grain rice
1½ tablespoons plain yogurt or kefir,
   for soaking
1 pound 2 ounces boneless leg of lamb,
   trimmed of fat and cut into chunks
¼ teaspoon saffron threads
3 tablespoons extra virgin olive oil
   or ghee
3 onions, halved and thinly sliced
1½ teaspoons fine sea salt
steamed snow peas, to serve

FOR THE MARINADE
¾ cup plain yogurt
1 tablespoon lemon juice or white
   wine vinegar
2 fresh green chilies, halved,
   seeded and thinly sliced
1 tablespoon grated ginger root
3 garlic cloves, crushed
1½ teaspoons ground cilantro
1 teaspoon paprika
¼ teaspoon turmeric
½ teaspoon ground cumin
½ teaspoon chili powder
¼ teaspoon ground cinnamon
¼ teaspoon ground cardamom
¼ teaspoon ground cloves
1 teaspoon fine sea salt

1 (6-9) (9-12) Put the rice, yogurt and 3½ cups water in a large saucepan and let soak, covered, 7 hours or overnight at room temperature.

2 To make the marinade, put all of the ingredients in a nonreactive bowl and mix well. Add the lamb and stir well, making sure the lamb is covered in the marinade. Cover and let marinate in the refrigerator 2 hours or overnight.

3 Put the saffron in a small bowl, cover with 1 tablespoon warm water and let soak. Heat the oil in a large, heavy-bottomed saucepan or flameproof casserole dish over medium heat. Add the onions and cook 5 minutes until beginning to brown, then turn the heat up to medium-high. Add the rice and soaking water, salt and the saffron mixture and bring to a boil over high heat, then turn the heat down to low.

4 Add the lamb and the marinade and simmer, covered, 1 hour until the lamb is tender and the rice is soft. Gently stir the lamb and rice together to make sure they are mixed well. Serve hot with steamed snow peas.

(6-9) LAMB, SNOW PEA & BROWN RICE PUREE
Put 4 tablespoons of the brown rice, 1 teaspoon of the yogurt and 1 cup water in a heavy-bottomed saucepan and let soak, covered, 7 hours or overnight at room temperature. Add 1¾ ounces of the lamb and bring to a boil over medium-high heat. Turn the heat down to low and simmer, covered, 50 minutes. Add 4 steamed snow peas and simmer, covered, 10 minutes longer until the lamb is completely cooked through and the rice is completely soft. Transfer to a blender and blend 30 seconds, adding water 1 teaspoon at a time, until smooth. Mix in 1 teaspoon of the oil and serve warm.

(9-12) LAMB STEW
Put 4 tablespoons of the brown rice, 1 teaspoon of the yogurt and 1 cup water in a heavy-bottomed saucepan and let soak, covered, 7 hours or overnight at room temperature. Add 1¾ ounces of the lamb, 1 teaspoon of the onion and a pinch of the garlic and bring to a boil over medium-high heat. Turn the heat down to low and simmer, covered, 50 minutes. Add 4 steamed snow peas and simmer, covered, 10 minutes longer until the lamb is completely cooked through and the rice is completely soft. Transfer to a blender and blend 15 seconds, adding water 1 teaspoon at a time, until the mixture forms a lumpy puree. Mix in 1 teaspoon of the oil and serve warm.

The lamb in this tagine is cooked slowly with a mix of spices, sweet orange juice, apricots and ginger. Leave it in the oven until all the flavors have married together and everything is tender —and really, really delicious.

Lamb Tagine

SERVES: 2 adults, 1 child and 1 baby
PREPARATION TIME: 45 minutes, plus at least 7 hours soaking and 20 minutes cooking the quinoa
COOKING TIME: 2½ to 3 hours
STORAGE: Refrigerate up to 1 day.

....

2 tablespoons extra virgin olive oil, plus extra for frying if needed
1 pound boneless lamb shoulder, trimmed of fat and cut into chunks
1 small onion, finely chopped
5 tablespoons freshly squeezed orange juice
7 ounces squash, seeded and cut into bite-size pieces, or pumpkin, peeled, seeded and cut into bite-size pieces
12 to 15 cherry tomatoes, halved
scant ⅔ cup dried unsulphured apricots, finely chopped
2 teaspoons grated ginger root
1 garlic clove, finely chopped
1 teaspoon ground cinnamon
¾ teaspoon ground cilantro
¼ teaspoon ground cloves
½ teaspoon paprika
½ teaspoon turmeric
½ teaspoon ground cumin
1 tablespoon wholegrain spelt flour or wholewheat flour
1 teaspoon fine sea salt
1 recipe quantity cooked quinoa (see page 22), to serve

1 Preheat the oven to 300°F. Heat the oil in a large, flameproof casserole dish over medium-high heat. (6-9) (9-12) Working in batches to avoid overcrowding the dish, add the lamb and cook, stirring frequently, 5 minutes until well browned on all sides. Remove from the dish, using a slotted spoon, and set aside. Repeat with the remaining lamb, adding more oil to the dish as needed.

2 Return the lamb to the dish. Add all of the remaining ingredients and 1 cup boiling water and mix well.

3 Transfer to the oven and bake, covered, 2 to 2½ hours until the lamb is completely tender. Serve hot over the cooked quinoa.

(6-9) LAMB, SQUASH, APRICOT & QUINOA PUREE
Put 1¾ ounces of the lamb, 6 squash pieces, 1 teaspoon of the apricots and 1 cup water in a casserole dish. Bake as above, covered, 20 minutes. Add 2 tablespoons of the cooked quinoa and bake, covered, 20 minutes longer until completely soft and the lamb is completely cooked through. Transfer to a blender and blend 30 seconds, adding water 1 teaspoon at a time, until smooth. Serve warm.

(9-12) LAMB & QUINOA STEW
Put 1¾ ounces of the lamb, 6 squash pieces, 1 teaspoon of the apricots, ½ teaspoon of the onion and 1 cup water in a casserole dish. Bake as above, covered, 20 minutes. Add 2 tablespoons of the cooked quinoa and bake, covered, 20 minutes longer until completely soft and the lamb is completely cooked through. Transfer to a blender and pulse 15 seconds, adding water 1 teaspoon at a time, until the mixture forms a lumpy puree. Serve warm.

Slowly Simmered Beef & Onion Stew

SERVES: 2 adults, 1 child and 1 baby
PREPARATION TIME: 30 minutes
COOKING TIME: 2½ hours
STORAGE: Refrigerate up to
1 day, or freeze up to 1 month.

. . . .

½ tablespoon wholegrain spelt flour
    or wholewheat flour
1 teaspoon fine sea salt
¼ teaspoon freshly ground black pepper
1 pound chuck steak, trimmed of fat
    and cut into chunks
1½ tablespoons extra virgin olive oil
2 large onions, halved and thinly sliced
1 garlic clove, finely chopped
½ teaspoon finely chopped thyme leaves
1 bay leaf
1 teaspoon finely chopped ginger root
6 tablespoons dark beer
1½ tablespoons cider vinegar or
    grape vinegar
1½ tablespoons chopped parsley leaves
steamed sweet potatoes, thickly sliced,
    to serve
steamed cauliflower, to serve

1 In a large bowl, mix together the flour, ½ teaspoon of the salt and the pepper. (6-9) (9-12) Add the beef and toss well, making sure the beef is coated in the flour mixture. Heat ½ tablespoon of the oil in a large, heavy-bottomed saucepan over medium-high heat. Working in batches to avoid overcrowding the pan, add the beef and cook 3 to 4 minutes on each side until well browned. Remove the beef from the pan, using a slotted spoon, transfer to a large bowl and set aside. Repeat with the remaining beef, adding another 1 teaspoon of oil to the pan before cooking each batch.

2 Reduce the heat to medium and add ½ tablespoon of the oil, the onions and the remaining salt. Cook, stirring occasionally, 5 minutes until the onions are beginning to brown. Add the garlic, thyme, bay leaf, ginger and 2 tablespoons water. Using a wooden spoon, lift the dark coating off the bottom of the pan. Cook 2 minutes, until all the brown coating has dissolved. Slowly add the beer and cider vinegar, then return the beef and any juices from the bowl to the pan.

3 Bring to a boil over medium-high heat, then turn the heat down to low and simmer, covered, 2 hours, stirring occasionally, until the beef is tender and cooked through. Remove the bay leaf and stir in the parsley. Serve hot with steamed sweet potatoes and cauliflower.

(6-9)

**FRIED BEEF & CAULIFLOWER PUREE
WITH MASHED SWEET POTATO**
Heat a heavy-bottomed skillet over medium heat until hot. Add 1¾ ounces of the beef and 3 steamed cauliflower florets and dry-fry, covered, 10 minutes until lightly browned and completely cooked through. Transfer to a blender and add 3 tablespoons water. Blend 30 seconds, adding extra water 1 teaspoon at a time, until smooth. Serve warm with mashed, steamed sweet potato.

(9-12)

**FRIED BEEF & VEGETABLES
WITH MASHED SWEET POTATO**
Heat a heavy-bottomed skillet over medium heat. Add 1¾ ounces of the beef, ½ slice of onion, 3 steamed cauliflower florets and a pinch of the garlic. Dry-fry, covered, 10 minutes until lightly browned and completely cooked through. Transfer to a blender and add 3 tablespoons water. Pulse 15 seconds, adding extra water 1 teaspoon at a time, until the mixture forms a lumpy puree. Serve warm with mashed, steamed sweet potato.

Louisiana Beef Grillade

SERVES: 2 adults, 1 child and 1 baby
PREPARATION TIME: 40 minutes
COOKING TIME: 1 hour 10 minutes
STORAGE: Refrigerate up to 1 day.

....

4 tablespoons wholegrain spelt flour
  or wholewheat flour
1½ teaspoons fine sea salt
4 tenderloin steaks, sliced into strips
3 tablespoons extra virgin olive oil
1 onion, quartered and thinly sliced
2 celery stalks, halved lengthwise
  and chopped
1 orange bell pepper, halved, seeded
  and diced
2 garlic cloves, finely chopped
1 cup beef stock
1¼ cups canned diced tomatoes
½ tablespoon finely chopped thyme
  leaves or ½ teaspoon dried thyme
½ tablespoon chopped basil leaves
  or ½ teaspoon dried basil
½ teaspoon crushed chilies
4 tablespoons chopped parsley leaves
1 cup grits or polenta
½ cup (1 stick) unsalted butter
freshly ground black pepper
steamed, shelled fava beans, to serve

1 Put 2 tablespoons of the flour and ½ teaspoon of the salt in a large, shallow bowl. (6-9) (9-12) Season with pepper and mix, then add the beef and toss well, making sure the beef is coated in the flour mixture.

2 Heat 2 tablespoons of the oil in a large, heavy-bottomed skillet over medium-high heat. Add the beef and cook, stirring frequently, 6 minutes until browned. Remove the beef from the skillet, using a slotted spoon, and set aside.

3 Add the remaining oil to the skillet, followed by the onion, celery and bell pepper. Cook, stirring occasionally, 5 minutes until tender. Stir in the garlic and the remaining flour and cook 5 minutes longer. Add the stock and 1 cup water and mix.

4 Return the beef to the skillet and add the canned tomatoes, thyme, basil, crushed chilies and parsley. Turn the heat down to low and simmer, covered, 45 to 50 minutes until the beef is completely tender.

5 Meanwhile, pour 4 cups water into a large saucepan and bring to a boil over high heat. Add the grits, whisking continuously with a whisk until smooth. Reduce the heat to medium-low and simmer, stirring continuously with a wooden spoon, 20 minutes until the grits are thick and rubbery. Remove from the heat, add the butter and the remaining salt and mix well. Serve hot with the beef and steamed fava beans.

(6-9) **BEEF & FAVA BEAN PUREE**
Heat a heavy-bottomed skillet over medium-high heat until hot. Add 1¾ ounces of the beef and 2 tablespoons of steamed fava beans and dry-fry 10 minutes until the beef is completely cooked through. Transfer to a blender and add 4 tablespoons water. Blend 30 seconds, adding extra water 1 teaspoon at a time, until smooth. Serve warm.

(9-12) **BEEF, FAVA BEAN, ONION & GRITS**
Heat a heavy-bottomed skillet over medium-high heat until hot. Add 1¾ ounces of the beef, 2 tablespoons of steamed fava beans, 1 teaspoon of the onion and a pinch of the parsley. Dry-fry 10 minutes until the beef is completely cooked through. Transfer to a blender and add 4 tablespoons of the cooked grits (without the butter or salt) and 4 tablespoons water. Pulse 15 seconds, adding extra water 1 teaspoon at a time, until the mixture forms a lumpy puree. Serve warm.

My sister Jan's husband is Egyptian and his mother taught her to make this delicious old-world family favorite. It's the Egyptian version of beef stew, which simmers slowly for a long time until the steak and celery almost melt away. With soul-warming potatoes, green beans and onion, it's the perfect fare for cold winter nights.

Egyptian Beef

SERVES: 2 adults, 1 child and 1 baby
PREPARATION TIME: 30 minutes, plus at least 7 hours soaking and 20 minutes cooking the buckwheat
COOKING TIME: 2 to 2½ hours
STORAGE: Refrigerate up to 1 day.

....

1 pound tenderloin roast, trimmed
    of fat and cut into chunks
½ teaspoon fine sea salt
¼ teaspoon freshly ground black pepper
1 onion, chopped
2 large celery stalks, halved lengthwise
    and chopped
2 cups chicken stock
1 large potato, quartered
    and sliced
8 ounces green beans
3½ tablespoons tomato paste
2 recipe quantities cooked buckwheat
    (see page 22), to serve

1 Heat a large, heavy-bottomed saucepan over medium-high heat until hot. (6-9) (9-12) Add the beef and cook, stirring occasionally, 6 minutes until browned. Add the salt and pepper and mix well.

2 Add the onion, celery and stock to the pan. Bring to a boil over medium-high heat, then turn the heat down to low and simmer, covered, 1½ to 2 hours until the celery and meat are meltingly tender.

3 Add the potato, green beans and tomato paste and cook 15 minutes longer or until the potatoes and beans are tender. Serve hot over the cooked buckwheat.

(6-9) **BEEF, GREEN BEANS & BUCKWHEAT PUREE**
Cut 1¾ ounces of the beef into small pieces, then cut 2 of the green beans into quarters. Put the beef and green beans in a saucepan, add 4 tablespoons of the cooked buckwheat and generous ½ cup water. Bring to a boil over medium-high heat, then turn the heat down to low and simmer, covered, 20 minutes until the beef is completely cooked through and the beans are completely soft. Transfer to a blender and add 3 tablespoons water. Blend 30 seconds, adding extra water 1 teaspoon at a time, until smooth. Serve warm.

(9-12) **BEEF, GREEN BEANS, ONION & BUCKWHEAT**
Cut 1¾ ounces of the beef into small pieces, then cut 2 of the green beans into quarters. Put the beef and green beans in a saucepan, add 4 tablespoons of the cooked buckwheat, 1 teaspoon of the onion and generous ½ cup water. Bring to a boil over medium-high heat, then turn the heat down to low and simmer, covered, 20 minutes until the beef is completely cooked through and the beans are completely soft. Transfer to a blender and add 3 tablespoons water. Pulse 15 seconds, adding extra water 1 teaspoon at a time, until the mixture forms a lumpy puree. Serve warm.

Chinese Beef Stir-Fry

SERVES: 2 adults, 1 child and 1 baby
PREPARATION TIME: 36 minutes, plus 1½ hours marinating, plus at least 7 hours soaking and 40 minutes cooking the brown rice
COOKING TIME: 20 minutes
STORAGE: Refrigerate up to 1 day.

....

3 tenderloin steaks, cut into chunks
2 tablespoons sesame oil
8 ounces broccoli, cut into bite-size florets
8 ounces cauliflower, cut into bite-size florets
1 recipe quantity cooked brown rice (see page 23), to serve

FOR THE MARINADE
3 tablespoons tamari soy sauce or shoyu soy sauce
2 tablespoons mirin
6 garlic cloves, finely chopped

FOR THE SAUCE
1 tablespoon cornstarch, ground arrowroot or crushed kuzu
½ cup vegetable stock
1½ tablespoons mirin
1 teaspoon tamari soy sauce or shoyu soy sauce
1 tablespoon toasted sesame oil
1½ teaspoons finely chopped ginger root

1 (9-18) To make the marinade, put all of the ingredients in a large, nonreactive bowl and mix well. (6-9) Add the beef and stir well, making sure the beef is covered in the marinade. Cover and let marinate in the refrigerator 1½ hours.

2 To make the sauce, mix the cornstarch and 1 tablespoon cold water together to make a smooth paste in a bowl. Add all of the remaining ingredients for the sauce and mix well.

3 Heat 1 tablespoon of the sesame oil in a wok or large skillet over medium-high heat. Using a slotted spoon, add the beef to the wok and reserve the marinade. Stir-fry over medium-high heat 6 minutes until browned. Remove the beef from the wok and set aside.

4 Reduce the heat to medium and add the remaining sesame oil. Add the marinade and bring to a boil. Cook 1 minute, then add the broccoli and cauliflower and cook, stirring occasionally, 5 minutes. Return the beef to the wok and add the sauce. Cook, stirring continuously, 3 minutes longer until the sauce has thickened, the beef is warmed through and the vegetables are just tender. Serve hot over the cooked brown rice.

(6-9) **BEEF, CAULIFLOWER, BROCCOLI & RICE PUREE**
Put 4 tablespoons of the cooked brown rice in a saucepan, add generous ½ cup boiling water and simmer, covered, over low heat 20 minutes until completely soft. Heat 1 teaspoon of the sesame oil in a wok. Add 1¾ ounces of the beef and 3 pieces each of the broccoli and cauliflower and cook 15 minutes until the beef is completely cooked through and the vegetables are completely soft. Transfer to a blender and add the rice and 3 tablespoons water. Blend 30 seconds, adding extra water 1 teaspoon at a time, until smooth. Serve warm.

(9-12) **GARLIC BEEF, CAULIFLOWER, BROCCOLI & BROWN RICE**
Put 4 tablespoons of the cooked brown rice in a saucepan, add generous ½ cup boiling water and simmer, covered, over low heat 20 minutes until completely soft. Heat 1 teaspoon of the sesame oil in a wok. Add 1¾ ounces of the beef, ½ teaspoon of the garlic and 3 pieces each of the broccoli and cauliflower and cook 15 minutes until the beef is completely cooked through and the vegetables are completely soft. Transfer to a blender and add the rice and 3 tablespoons water. Pulse 15 seconds, adding extra water 1 teaspoon at a time, until the mixture forms a lumpy puree. Serve warm.

The flavors are simple, but great. When you serve this with sweet potatoes, you enjoy an excellent source of beta-carotene to raise blood levels of vitamin A, which is important for growth in children.

Herb-Crusted Fish

SERVES: 2 adults, 1 child and 1 baby
PREPARATION TIME: 15 minutes
COOKING TIME: 13 minutes
STORAGE: Refrigerate up to 1 day.

....

5½ ounces boneless salmon fillets
5½ ounces boneless sea bream fillets
1 tablespoon wholegrain spelt flour or
    wholewheat flour, for dusting
1½ tablespoons extra virgin olive oil,
    plus extra for greasing
3 tablespoons lime or lemon juice
2 tablespoons dried wholewheat
    breadcrumbs
½ scallion, finely chopped
1 garlic clove, finely chopped
1 tablespoon chopped parsley leaves
1 tablespoon finely chopped thyme
    leaves or 1 teaspoon dried thyme
¼ teaspoon fine sea salt
4 large, baked sweet potatoes, to serve
10½ ounces steamed, shelled fava
    beans, to serve
lemon wedges, to serve

1 (6-9) (9-18) Preheat the oven to 400°F and grease a baking dish with oil. Coat the flesh (not the skin side) of the fish fillets in flour to make a dry surface for the herb mixture to stick to. Shake off any excess flour and transfer, skin-side down, to the baking dish.

2 Put the oil, lime juice, breadcrumbs, scallion, garlic, parsley, thyme and salt in a small bowl and mix well. Spread the herb mixture evenly over the top of each fish.

3 Bake about 10 minutes until the salmon is opaque and cooked through and the sea bream is white and flaky, then preheat the broiler to medium-high. Put the fish under the broiler 3 minutes until the topping is golden brown. Serve hot with the baked sweet potatoes, steamed fava beans and lemon wedges.

(6-9) **SALMON, FAVA BEAN & SWEET POTATO PUREE**
Remove the skin and rub oil over 1¾ ounces of the salmon. Transfer to a baking dish and add 2 tablespoons of steamed fava beans and 2 tablespoons water. Bake as above 10 minutes until the salmon is opaque and completely cooked through. Transfer to a blender and add 2 tablespoons of baked sweet potato flesh and 3 tablespoons water. Blend 30 seconds, adding extra water 1 teaspoon at a time, until smooth. Serve warm.

 HERBED SALMON WITH FAVA BEANS & SWEET POTATO
Remove the skin and rub oil over 1¾ ounces of the salmon. Transfer to a baking dish and add 2 tablespoons of steamed fava beans and 2 tablespoons water. Sprinkle with 1 teaspoon of the scallion and a pinch each of the garlic and parsley and bake as above 10 minutes until the salmon is opaque and completely cooked through. Transfer to a blender and add 2 tablespoons of baked sweet potato flesh and 3 tablespoons water. Pulse 15 seconds, adding extra water 1 teaspoon at a time, until the mixture forms a lumpy puree. Serve warm.

Fragrant and succulent, this combines beautiful flavors from the fish, vegetables and spices. You can lift it out of the pot gently to keep the potatoes intact or break it up for a dense, chunky stew. It's a complete meal on its own, but it's also good served with pita bread to mop up the sauce.

Moroccan Fish

SERVES: 2 adults, 1 child and 1 baby
PREPARATION TIME: 35 minutes, plus at least 7 hours soaking and 40 minutes cooking the brown rice
COOKING TIME: 30 minutes
STORAGE: Refrigerate up to 1 day.

....

4 tablespoons extra virgin olive oil, plus extra to serve
2 onions, finely sliced
4 potatoes, finely sliced
4 carrots, sliced
6 plum tomatoes, sliced
8 garlic cloves, sliced
5½ ounces boneless, skinless haddock or pollock fillets, cut into chunks
5½ ounces boneless, skinless salmon fillets, cut into chunks
2 tablespoons finely chopped cilantro leaves
1 teaspoon ground cumin
1 teaspoon paprika
1½ teaspoons fine sea salt
1 recipe quantity cooked brown rice (see page 23), to serve

1 Put 2 tablespoons of the oil in a large, heavy-bottomed skillet with a tight-fitting lid. **(9-12)** Arrange the onions in a layer on the bottom of the skillet. **(6-9)** Add 2 layers of the potatoes, followed by the carrots, tomatoes and garlic. Put the fish on top of the vegetables and pour in the remaining oil. Sprinkle the cilantro, cumin, paprika and salt over the top of the fish.

2 Cook, covered, over medium heat 20 to 30 minutes until the haddock is white and flaky, the salmon is opaque and cooked through, the potatoes are soft and the juices from the fish and the vegetables have combined to form a sauce. Serve with the cooked brown rice.

(6-9) SALMON, CARROT & BROWN RICE PUREE
Put 4 tablespoons of the cooked brown rice, 2 tablespoons of the carrots and generous ½ cup boiling water in a saucepan and simmer, covered, 10 minutes. Add 1¾ ounces of the salmon and cook 10 minutes longer until the salmon is opaque and completely cooked through and the carrots are completely soft. Transfer to a blender and add 4 tablespoons water. Blend 30 seconds, adding extra water 1 teaspoon at a time, until smooth. Mix in 1 teaspoon of the oil and serve warm.

(9-12) SALMON WITH VEGGIES & BROWN RICE
Put 4 tablespoons of the cooked brown rice, 2 tablespoons of the carrots and generous ½ cup boiling water in a saucepan and simmer, covered, 10 minutes. Add 1¾ ounces of the salmon and 1 teaspoon of the onion and cook 10 minutes longer until the salmon is opaque and completely cooked through and the vegetables are completely soft. Transfer to a blender and add 4 tablespoons water. Pulse 15 seconds, adding extra water 1 teaspoon at a time, until the mixture forms a lumpy puree. Mix in 1 teaspoon of the oil and serve warm.

Fish Pie

SERVES: 2 adults, 1 child and 1 baby
PREPARATION TIME: 40 minutes,
plus 30 minutes chilling
COOKING TIME: 1 hour
STORAGE: Refrigerate up to 1 day.

....

unsalted butter, for greasing
1 large sweet potato, diced
1 large potato, diced
1 carrot, halved lengthwise and sliced
7 ounces boneless, skinless pollock
   or hake fillets, cut into chunks
7 ounces boneless, skinless salmon
   fillets, cut into chunks
5 shallots, chopped
salad, to serve

FOR THE DOUGH
1 cup wholegrain spelt flour or
   wholewheat flour, plus extra
   for dusting
¼ teaspoon fine sea salt
4½ tablespoons chilled, unsalted
   butter, diced

FOR THE SAUCE
3 tablespoons extra virgin olive oil
3 tablespoons wholegrain spelt flour
   or wholewheat flour
generous 1 cup vegetable stock
2 teaspoons chopped rosemary leaves
½ teaspoon fine sea salt

1 To make the dough, mix the flour and salt in a large bowl and rub in the butter with your fingertips until the mixture resembles breadcrumbs. Sprinkle 3 to 4 tablespoons cold water into the mixture, 1 tablespoon at a time, and mix with a fork until the dough is beginning to hold together. Shape the dough into a ball, wrap in plastic wrap and chill in the refrigerator 30 minutes.

2 Preheat the oven to 400°F and grease a 10-inch pie plate with butter. (6-9) (9-12) Meanwhile, put the potatoes and carrot in a steamer and steam, covered, 10 minutes until just tender. Put the potatoes, carrot, fish and shallots in a large bowl and mix well.

3 To make the sauce, mix the oil and flour in a heavy-bottomed saucepan and cook, stirring continuously, over medium heat 1 minute. Remove the pan from the heat and gradually add the stock, rosemary and salt. Return the pan to medium-low heat and cook, stirring continuously, 5 minutes until thickened and smooth.

4 Add the sauce to the fish mixture and mix well. Pour the mixture into the pie plate and smooth the top with the back of a wooden spoon. Dust a piece of parchment paper with flour. Roll out the dough into a circle about 10 inches in diameter and trim around the edges, using a sharp knife, to neaten. Ease the dough onto the top of the pie plate and cover the filling, then press down around the rim of the pie plate with your fingers to seal and crimp the edge. Using a sharp knife, cut a small cross in the centre of the dough lid. Bake 40 minutes until the pie is golden brown. Serve warm with salad.

(6-9) SALMON, SWEET POTATO & CARROT PUREE
Finely chop 2 tablespoons each of the carrot and sweet potato. Transfer to a ramekin and add 1¾ ounces of the salmon and 2 tablespoons water. Bake as above 15 minutes until the salmon is opaque and completely cooked through. Transfer to a blender and add 3 tablespoons water. Blend 30 seconds, adding extra water 1 teaspoon at a time, until smooth. Serve warm.

(9-12) POLLOCK WITH SWEET POTATO, SHALLOTS & CARROTS
Finely chop 1 tablespoon of the carrot and 2 tablespoons of the sweet potato. Transfer to a ramekin and add 1¾ ounces of the pollock, 2 shallot pieces and 2 tablespoons water. Bake as above 15 minutes until the pollock is completely cooked through. Transfer to a blender and add 3 tablespoons water. Pulse 15 seconds, adding extra water 1 teaspoon at a time, until the mixture forms a lumpy puree. Serve warm.

Packed with flavor and fresh, bright vegetables, here's a meal that's beautiful to see and to eat. Whenever I make this dish, my friends always ask for the recipe—it's a true crowd-pleaser.

Noodles with Saucy Squid

SERVES: 2 adults, 1 child and 1 baby
PREPARATION TIME: 35 minutes
COOKING TIME: 10 minutes
STORAGE: Refrigerate up to 1 day.

....

2 tablespoons extra virgin olive oil
1 carrot, cut into matchsticks
1 small yellow bell pepper, halved, seeded and cut into matchsticks
1 small red bell pepper, halved, seeded and cut into matchsticks
1 zucchini, cut into matchsticks
½ cup defrosted, frozen peas or fresh, podded peas
4 tablespoons lemon juice
5 tablespoons dry white wine
10½ ounces squid tubes, cut into rings
10½ ounces 100 percent buckwheat soba noodles or brown rice noodles

FOR THE SAUCE
3 garlic cloves, chopped
2 tablespoons extra virgin olive oil
4 tablespoons chopped basil leaves, 4 tablespoons grated Parmesan cheese and ¼ teaspoon fine sea salt or 8 tablespoons unsweetened, dried flaked coconut and 1 teaspoon fine sea salt

1 (6-9) (9-12) To make the sauce, mix all of the ingredients in a small bowl, then cover and set aside.

2 Heat the oil in a wok or large skillet over medium-high heat. Add the carrot and stir-fry 3 minutes, then add the bell peppers and zucchini and stir-fry 2 minutes longer. Add the peas and stir-fry 1 minute until the carrot and bell peppers are tender but remain crunchy. Remove the vegetables from the skillet and transfer to a large bowl. Sprinkle with the lemon juice and mix well.

3 Add the wine to the wok and bring to a boil over high heat. Reduce the heat to medium and add the squid. Simmer 3 minutes until the squid is just cooked and tender. Add the sauce and mix well.

4 Meanwhile, cook the noodles in plenty of boiling water, according to the package directions, and drain well. Serve warm topped with the saucy squid and vegetables.

(6-9) **CARROT, ZUCCHINI, COCONUT, PEA & NOODLE PUREE**
Put 1½ tablespoons each of the carrot, zucchini and peas in a steamer and steam, covered, 10 minutes until completely soft. Transfer to a blender and add 2 tablespoons of chopped, cooked noodles (without the saucy squid), 1 tablespoon of the coconut and 3 tablespoons water. Blend 30 seconds, adding extra water 1 teaspoon at a time, until smooth. Mix in 1 teaspoon of the oil and serve warm.

 NOODLES WITH VEG & COCONUT
Put 1 tablespoon each of the carrot, zucchini and peas in a steamer and steam, covered, 10 minutes until completely soft. Transfer to a blender and add 2 tablespoons of chopped, cooked noodles (without the saucy squid), 1 tablespoon of the coconut and 3 tablespoons water. Pulse 15 seconds, adding extra water 1 teaspoon at a time, until the mixture forms a lumpy puree. Mix in 1 teaspoon of the oil and serve warm.

My brother David has perfected this dish over the years and is sweet enough to make it for me when we are home for the holidays. He serves it as an appetizer, but I also love it over rice as a main meal. Spiced with jalapeño and chili, it also has lime and cumin, which are heavenly.

Spicy Avocado Shrimp

SERVES: 2 adults, 1 child and 1 baby
PREPARATION TIME: 20 minutes
COOKING TIME: 10 minutes
STORAGE: Use the same day.

....

10½ ounces brown rice noodles
1 teaspoon fine sea salt
6 tablespoons extra virgin olive oil
8 ounces raw, peeled jumbo shrimp
3 to 4 tablespoons lime juice
1 teaspoon fine lime zest
2 avocados, peeled, pitted and cut
    into bite-size pieces
3 to 4 plum tomatoes, chopped
1 small red onion, finely chopped
1 small jalapeño pepper, halved,
    seeded and finely chopped
4 tablespoons chopped cilantro leaves
1 tablespoon ground cumin
½ teaspoon chili powder

1 Cook the noodles in plenty of boiling water, according to the package directions. (6-9) (9-12) Drain the noodles, add the salt and toss well.

2 Meanwhile, heat 2 tablespoons of the oil in a large skillet over medium heat. Add the shrimp and fry, turning occasionally, 3 minutes until opaque and pink. Transfer to a large bowl, add the remaining ingredients and mix well. Stir in the noodles and mix thoroughly. Serve warm.

(6-9)

RICE NOODLES & AVOCADO PUREE
Put 4 tablespoons of chopped, cooked noodles (drained and without the salt), 6 avocado pieces and 3 tablespoons water in a blender. Blend 30 seconds, adding extra water 1 teaspoon at a time, until smooth. Serve warm.

(9-12)

SPICED RICE NOODLES WITH AVOCADO
Put 4 tablespoons of chopped, cooked noodles, (drained and without the salt), 6 avocado pieces, a pinch of the cilantro and 3 tablespoons water in a blender. Pulse 15 seconds, adding extra water 1 teaspoon at a time, until the mixture forms a lumpy puree. Serve warm.

Scallops with Spicy Black Bean Sauce

SERVES: 2 adults, 1 child and 1 baby
PREPARATION TIME: 35 minutes, plus 30 minutes marinating, plus at least 12 hours soaking and 1 hour 40 minutes cooking the black beans (optional), plus at least 7 hours soaking and 40 minutes cooking the brown rice
COOKING TIME: 25 minutes
STORAGE: Refrigerate the scallops for up to 1 day. Refrigerate the sauce and brown rice up to 3 days.

....

12 ounces shelled scallops
2 tablespoons toasted sesame oil
1 onion, finely chopped
1 bell pepper, halved, seeded and finely sliced
1 recipe quantity cooked dried black beans (see page 23) or 1½ cups drained and rinsed canned black (turtle) beans
½ teaspoon fine sea salt
8 ounces sweet peas, trimmed
1 recipe quantity cooked brown rice or cooked wild rice (see page 23), to serve

FOR THE MARINADE
2 tablespoons finely chopped ginger root
3 garlic cloves, finely chopped
2 tablespoons tamari soy sauce or shoyu soy sauce
1 teaspoon toasted sesame oil

FOR THE SAUCE
1 cup vegetable stock
3 tablespoons mirin

1 To make the marinade, mix together all of the ingredients in a large, nonreactive bowl. Rinse and carefully pat the scallops dry with paper towels. Add the scallops to the marinade and stir well, making sure the scallops are covered in the marinade. Cover and let marinate in the refrigerator 30 minutes.

2 To make the sauce, put the ingredients in a bowl and mix well.

3 Heat 1 tablespoon of the oil in a large skillet over medium-high heat until hot but not smoking. Using a slotted spoon, add the scallops to the skillet and reserve the marinade. Cook 4 to 5 minutes on each side until they are opaque and firm. Remove from the skillet, using a slotted spoon, and transfer to a plate. (6-9) (9-12) Reduce the heat to medium and heat the remaining oil in the skillet. Add the onion and bell pepper and cook, stirring occasionally, 5 minutes until just tender.

4 Put the cooked black beans in a bowl with the salt. (Add the kombu, if used during cooking.) Coarsely mash the beans and add to the skillet, then add the snow peas, sauce and the reserved marinade. Cook 5 minutes until the snow peas are soft. Return the scallops to the skillet and cook 2 minutes until they have warmed through. Serve hot over the cooked brown rice.

(6-9) BROWN RICE, BLACK BEAN & SNOW PEA PUREE
Put 4 tablespoons of the cooked brown rice and generous ½ cup boiling water in a saucepan and simmer, covered, over low heat 10 minutes. Add 4 snow peas and cook 10 minutes longer until completely soft. Transfer to a blender and add 2 tablespoons of the cooked black bleans and 4 tablespoons water. Blend 30 seconds, adding extra water 1 teaspoon at a time, until smooth. Mix in 1 teaspoon of the oil and serve warm.

(9-12) BROWN RICE, BLACK BEAN, SNOW PEA & ONION
Put 4 tablespoons of the cooked brown rice and generous ½ cup boiling water in a saucepan and simmer, covered, over low heat 10 minutes. Add 4 snow peas and 1 teaspoon of the onion and cook 10 minutes longer until completely soft. Transfer to a blender and add 2 tablespoons of the cooked black beans and 4 tablespoons water. Pulse 15 seconds, adding extra water 1 teaspoon at a time, until the mixture forms a lumpy puree. Mix in 1 teaspoon of the oil and serve warm.

Quiche is great—especially when you don't bother with the crust. We love the lift that the mustard gives this, and using yogurt instead of milk or cream is a great habit to get into. My sister, Jan, gave me a version of this recipe when I left home and first started cooking.

Broccoli Pecorino Quiche

SERVES: 2 adults, 1 child and 1 baby
PREPARATION TIME: 30 minutes
COOKING TIME: 40 minutes
STORAGE: Refrigerate up to 1 day.

....

unsalted butter, for greasing
6 extra-large eggs
scant 1½ cups plain yogurt
5½ ounces Pecorino cheese, grated
1½ tablespoons Dijon mustard
5 tablespoons wholegrain spelt flour
    or wholewheat flour
1½ teaspoons finely chopped
    thyme leaves
½ teaspoon fine sea salt
6 ounces broccoli, stems peeled
    and sliced and florets cut into
    bite-size pieces
1 onion, finely chopped
salad, to serve
cooked brown rice pasta,
    millet pasta, quinoa pasta or
    buckwheat pasta, any shape,
    to serve
extra virgin olive oil, to serve

1 Preheat the oven to 350°F and grease a 10-inch pie plate with butter. In a large bowl, lightly beat the eggs together with a whisk. **(9-12)** Add the yogurt, Pecorino, mustard, flour, thyme and salt and whisk. **(6-9)** Put the broccoli and onion in the bottom of the pie plate and pour the egg mixture over the top.

2 Bake 35 to 40 minutes until cooked through and the edges have browned. Serve with salad and pasta tossed with oil.

(6-9) PASTA & BROCCOLI PUREE
Put 9 broccoli pieces in a steamer and steam, covered, 10 minutes until completely soft. Transfer to a blender and add 4 tablespoons of chopped, cooked pasta and 3 tablespoons water. Blend 30 seconds, adding extra water 1 teaspoon at a time, until smooth. Serve warm.

(9-12) PASTA, BROCCOLI & ONION WITH YOGURT
Put 6 broccoli pieces and 1 teaspoon of the onion in a steamer and steam, covered, 10 minutes until completely soft. Transfer to a blender and add 4 tablespoons of chopped, cooked pasta and 3 tablespoons water. Pulse 15 seconds, adding extra water 1 teaspoon at a time, until the mixture forms a lumpy puree. Mix in 2 tablespoons of the yogurt and serve warm.

Mashed miso sweet potatoes is one of my favorite ways to eat sweet potatoes and another great way to use miso. This version of shepherd's pie combines mashed potatoes and sweet potatoes with creamy lentils that are delicately sweetened with mirin.

Vegetarian Shepherd's Pie

SERVES: 2 adults, 1 child and 1 baby
PREPARATION TIME: 30 minutes, plus at least 7 hours soaking the brown lentils
COOKING TIME: 1½ hours
STORAGE: Refrigerate up to 3 days.

....

1 recipe quantity soaked brown
    lentils (see page 25)
1 strip of kombu, 6¼ x 4 inches, finely
    cut with scissors (optional)
1 tomato, chopped
1 parsnip, quartered lengthwise
    and sliced
1 carrot, quartered lengthwise and
    sliced
1 small leek, quartered lengthwise
    and sliced
6 garlic cloves, roughly chopped
2 tablespoons chopped parsley leaves
1 teaspoon finely chopped thyme leaves
2 tablespoons mirin
1 teaspoon fine sea salt
2 tablespoons extra virgin olive oil,
    plus extra for greasing
salad, to serve

FOR THE MASHED MISO POTATOES
2 large potatoes, cut into chunks
1 sweet potato, cut into chunks
2 tablespoons miso, any variety
6 tablespoons extra virgin olive oil

1 (6-9) (9-18) Put the soaked brown lentils in a large saucepan, add 2⅔ cups water and bring to a boil over high heat. Boil 10 minutes, skimming any scum that rises to the surface, then turn the heat down to low and add the kombu, if using. Simmer, covered, 25 minutes, then add the tomato, parsnip, carrot, leek, garlic, parsley and thyme and simmer, covered, 10 minutes longer. Add the mirin, salt and oil and mix well. Remove from the heat.

2 Preheat the oven to 350°F and grease an 8 x 12-inch or equivalent baking dish with oil. To make the mashed potatoes, put the potatoes in a steamer and steam, covered, 20 to 25 minutes until soft. Remove the potatoes from the steamer and reserve ½ cup of the steaming water. Put the miso and the reserved steaming water in a bowl and stir until the miso has completely dissolved. Add the potatoes and oil and mash until smooth.

3 Pour the lentil mixture into the baking dish, then spread the mashed potatoes on top and smooth the surface with a spatula. Bake 25 minutes until bubbling and golden brown on top. Serve hot with salad.

(6-9) SWEET POTATO, PARSNIP & LENTIL PUREE
Put 6 sweet potato pieces, 1 tablespoon of the parsnip, 2 tablespoons of the soaked brown lentils and ¾ cup water in a saucepan. Simmer, covered, over low heat 45 minutes until completely soft. Transfer to a blender and blend 30 seconds, adding water 1 teaspoon at a time, until smooth. Mix in 1 teaspoon of the oil and serve warm.

(9-12) SWEET POTATO, PARSNIP, LENTIL, LEEK, GARLIC & PARSLEY
Put 6 sweet potato pieces, 1 tablespoon of the parsnip, 2 tablespoons of the soaked brown lentils, 1 teaspoon of the leek, 1 garlic piece, a pinch of the parsley and ¾ cup water in a saucepan. Simmer, covered, over low heat 45 minutes until completely soft. Transfer to a blender and pulse 15 seconds, adding water 1 teaspoon at a time, until the mixture forms a lumpy puree. Mix in 1 teaspoon of the oil and serve warm.

Pot Pie with Cheesy Polenta

SERVES: 2 adults, 1 child and 1 baby
PREPARATION TIME: 30 minutes,
plus 10 minutes setting
COOKING TIME: 50 minutes
STORAGE: Refrigerate up to 3 days.

....

2 tablespoons extra virgin olive oil,
    plus extra for greasing
1 potato, diced
3 shallots, chopped
5 tablespoons wholegrain spelt flour
    or wholewheat flour
generous 1½ cups vegetable stock
½ cup plain yogurt
2 garlic cloves, crushed
2 tablespoons chopped parsley leaves
1 teaspoon finely chopped sage leaves
½ teaspoon finely chopped thyme leaves
a large pinch of cayenne pepper
5½ ounces asparagus, chopped
2 carrots, halved lengthwise and sliced
⅔ cup defrosted, frozen peas or fresh,
    podded peas
scant ⅔ cup instant polenta
2½ ounces cheddar cheese, grated
½ teaspoon fine sea salt
salad, to serve

1 Preheat the oven to 400°F and grease a 10-inch pie plate with oil. Heat the oil in a large saucepan over medium heat. Add the potato and shallots and sprinkle the flour over the top. Cook, stirring frequently, 5 minutes until the flour has lightly browned. Pour in the stock, then add the yogurt, garlic, parsley, sage, thyme and cayenne pepper and cook, stirring frequently, 5 minutes until the sauce has thickened.

2 Add the asparagus, carrots and peas to the saucepan and mix well. Pour the vegetable mix into the pie plate and level the surface with the back of a wooden spoon.

3 In a large, heavy-bottomed saucepan, bring scant 2 cups water to a boil over high heat. Pour the polenta in a stream, whisking continuously with a whisk until smooth. Turn the heat down to low and simmer, stirring continuously with a wooden spoon, 5 minutes until the polenta is thick and rubbery but loose enough to spread. Remove from the heat and mix in the cheddar cheese and salt until well combined.

4 Spread the cheesy polenta on top of the vegetables in the pie plate and smooth the surface with a spatula. Cut a few small air holes through the polenta, using a sharp knife, and bake 30 to 35 minutes until bubbling and golden brown on top. Remove from the oven and let rest to set 10 minutes. Serve hot with salad.

CARROT & PEA PUREE
Put 2½ tablespoons of the carrots in a steamer and steam, covered, 10 minutes. Add 2½ tablespoons of the peas and steam, covered, 10 minutes longer until completely soft. Transfer to a blender and add 3 tablespoons water. Blend 30 seconds, adding extra water 1 teaspoon at a time, until smooth. Serve warm.

POLENTA WITH VEGETABLES & YOGURT
Put 1 tablespoon of the carrots in a steamer and steam, covered, 10 minutes. Add 1 tablespoon each of the asparagus, shallots and peas and steam 10 minutes longer until completely soft. Transfer to a blender and add 2 tablespoons water. Pulse 15 seconds, adding extra water 1 teaspoon at a time, until the mixture forms a lumpy puree. Mix in 2 tablespoons of the yogurt and serve warm with 2 tablespoons of the cooked polenta (without the cheese or salt).

We love quesadilla—and here's a different version. It's not covered with a tortilla, so you can load it up with great toppings. As long as the bottom tortilla has browned, it will hold the weight of all of the ingredients. This is good fresh and hot, or the next day without the toppings in your child's lunch bag.

Open Quesadilla with Salsa

SERVES: 2 adults, 1 child and 1 baby
PREPARATION TIME: 25 minutes, plus at least 12 hours soaking and 1 hour 40 minutes cooking the pinto beans (optional)
COOKING TIME: 30 minutes
STORAGE: Refrigerate up to 3 days.

....

1 recipe quantity cooked dried pinto beans (see page 25) or 3 cups drained and rinsed canned pinto beans
1 teaspoon fine sea salt
1½ cups frozen corn kernels
6 wholegrain tortillas
6¼ ounces cheddar cheese, grated
1 avocado, peeled, pitted and chopped

FOR THE SALSA
3 tomatoes, coarsely chopped
1 small red onion, chopped
1 to 1½ jalapeño peppers, halved, seeded and finely chopped
1 tablespoon lemon juice
1 garlic clove, crushed
¼ teaspoon fine sea salt

1 (6-9) (9-12) Mix the cooked pinto beans and salt in a large bowl and set aside.

2 Put the corn kernels in a steamer and steam, covered, 3 to 4 minutes until just tender.

3 To make the salsa, put all of the ingredients in a bowl and mix well.

4 Heat a large, heavy-bottomed skillet over medium-low heat until hot. Put 1 tortilla in the skillet and sprinkle with 1 ounce of the cheddar cheese, followed by ½ cup of the cooked pinto beans. Cook 3 to 4 minutes until the bottom of the tortilla has lightly browned and the cheese has melted. Slide a large spatula under the tortilla and transfer to a plate. Top with the corn kernels, avocado and salsa and cut into slices. Repeat with the remaining tortillas and serve warm.

(6-9) PINTO BEAN & AVOCADO PUREE
Put 2 tablespoons of the cooked pinto beans and 6 avocado pieces in a blender. Blend 30 seconds, adding water 1 teaspoon at a time, until smooth. Serve warm.

(9-12) PINTO BEAN, AVOCADO, ONION & GARLIC
Put 1 teaspoon of the onion, a pinch of the garlic and 1 tablespoon boiling water in a skillet and cook over medium-high heat 3 to 4 minutes until completely soft. Transfer to a blender and add 2 tablespoons of the cooked pinto beans and 6 avocado pieces. Pulse 15 seconds, adding water 1 teaspoon at a time, until the mixture forms a lumpy puree. Serve warm.

Lentils with rice is always nice, but this is pretty dreamy. It's lovely winter food, warm and filling with the lentils creamy and soft on top of potatoes that are accented with sauce and extra virgin olive oil.

Creamy Lentils & Mashed Potatoes

SERVES: 2 adults, 1 child and 1 baby
PREPARATION TIME: 25 minutes, plus at least 7 hours soaking the lentils
COOKING TIME: 1 hour
STORAGE: Refrigerate up to 3 days.

....

1 recipe quantity soaked Puy lentils (see page 25)
2 carrots, sliced
1 strip of kombu, 6¼ x 4 inches (optional)
½ cup extra virgin olive oil, plus extra to serve
1 onion, chopped
6 garlic cloves, chopped
3½ ounces fresh or defrosted, frozen spinach, chopped
2 teaspoons fine sea salt
1 pound 2 ounces potatoes, diced
1 pound 2 ounces sweet potatoes, diced
3 tablespoons Worcestershire sauce

1 Put the soaked Puy lentils, carrots and 3½ cups water in a large saucepan. Bring to a boil over high heat, skimming any scum that rises to the surface, then turn the heat down to low and add the kombu, if using. Simmer, covered, 45 minutes. Remove the kombu from the pan, chop and set aside. **(6-9) (9-12)**

2 Heat 2 tablespoons of the oil in a large, heavy-bottomed skillet over medium heat. Add the onion and garlic and cook 5 minutes until beginning to brown. Add the onion, garlic and spinach to the lentils and simmer, covered, 10 minutes longer. Add the chopped kombu, if using, and 1½ teaspoons of the salt and mix well.

3 Meanwhile, put the potatoes in a steamer and steam, covered, 15 minutes until completely soft. Remove from the heat, transfer to a large bowl and mash until smooth. Add the Worcestershire sauce and the remaining oil and salt and mix well. Serve the lentils hot over the mashed potatoes with a drizzle of oil.

(6-9)

PUY LENTIL, CARROT & SWEET POTATO PUREE
Put 3 tablespoons of the cooked Puy lentils and carrots, 2 tablespoons of the steamed sweet potato and 3 tablespoons water in a blender. Blend 30 seconds, adding extra water 1 teaspoon at a time, until smooth. Mix in 1 teaspoon of the oil and serve warm.

(9-12)

PUY LENTIL, CARROT, SWEET POTATO, ONION & GARLIC STEW
Put 5 tablespoons each of the cooked Puy lentils and carrots, 2 tablespoons of the steamed sweet potato, 1 teaspoon of the cooked onion and garlic mixture and 3 tablespoons water in a blender. Pulse 15 seconds, adding extra water 1 teaspoon at a time, until the mixture forms a lumpy puree. Mix in 1 teaspoon of the oil and serve warm.

When my sister Jan and her kids arrived last July for a one-month visit, I greeted them with these. Everyone ate them so quickly that I could hardly keep up in the kitchen. They are deliciously crispy—lovely with the creamy yogurt sauce.

Lentil Fritters with Yogurt Sauce

MAKES: 12
PREPARATION TIME: 35 minutes, plus at least 12 hours soaking and 30 minutes cooking the large green lentils
COOKING TIME: 30 minutes
STORAGE: Refrigerate up to 3 days.

....

2 extra-large eggs
2 teaspoons fine sea salt
a large pinch of cayenne pepper
3 tablespoons chopped parsley leaves
3 tablespoons lemon juice
3 garlic cloves, crushed
1 small parsnip or carrot, grated
1 small onion, finely chopped
2½ ounces frozen spinach, finely chopped
2 to 3 tablespoons wholegrain spelt flour or wholewheat flour, plus extra for dusting
½ cup rolled oats
1 recipe quantity cooked large green lentils (see page 25)
4 tablespoons extra virgin olive oil, plus extra to serve
cooked pasta, any type, any shape, to serve

FOR THE YOGURT SAUCE
1 cup plain yogurt
2 tablespoons Worcestershire sauce
2 tablespoons lemon juice

1 In a large mixing bowl, lightly beat the eggs together with a whisk. (6-9) (9-12) Add the salt, cayenne pepper, parsley, lemon juice, garlic, parsnip, onion, spinach, flour and oats and mix well. Add the cooked large green lentils and mix until well combined.

2 To make the sauce, put all of the ingredients in a small bowl and mix well.

3 Heat 2 tablespoons of the oil in a large, heavy-bottomed skillet over medium-low heat. Working in batches, scoop the mixture by the tablespoon into your hand and shape it into a fritter. They need to be handled gently and they won't hold together well in your hand, but they do in the skillet. Flip your hand over so the fritter lands in the skillet and cook 5 minutes on each side until they are crisp and golden brown. Repeat with the remaining fritters, adding the remaining oil to the skillet as needed. Serve hot with the yogurt sauce and pasta tossed with oil.

(6-9) LENTIL & PARSNIP PUREE
Put 4 tablespoons of the cooked large green lentils, 1 tablespoon of the parsnip and 3 tablespoons water in a blender. Blend 30 seconds, adding extra water 1 teaspoon at a time, until smooth. Mix in 1 teaspoon of the oil and serve warm.

(9-12) YOGURT, LENTIL, PARSNIP & PARSLEY
Put 2 tablespoons of the yogurt, 2 tablespoons of the cooked large green lentils, 1 tablespoon of the parsnip, a pinch of the parsley and 2 tablespoons water in a blender. Pulse 15 seconds, adding extra water 1 teaspoon at a time, until the mixture forms a lumpy puree. Mix in 1 teaspoon of the oil and serve warm.

This is the first baked stuffed squash I ever made and it's a huge hit. The flavors are perfectly balanced and it is a healthy, beautiful dish. Enjoy it as a weekend treat or serve it at festive occasions.

Baked Stuffed Squash

SERVES: 2 adults, 1 child and 1 baby
PREPARATION TIME: 30 minutes
COOKING TIME: 1 hour 10 minutes
STORAGE: Refrigerate up to 3 days.

....

⅓ cup pine nuts
1 butternut squash, halved and seeded
4¼ ounces goat cheese, crumbled
1 fennel bulb, diced
1 leek, quartered lengthwise
    and sliced
1 garlic clove, crushed
2 tablespoons chopped parsley leaves
½ teaspoon finely chopped thyme leaves
½ cup extra virgin olive oil
1 teaspoon fine sea salt
10½ ounces brown rice pasta,
    millet pasta, quinoa pasta or
    buckwheat pasta, any shape
avocado salad, to serve

1 Preheat the broiler to medium. Put the pine nuts on a baking sheet and broil 1 to 2 minutes until lightly browned.

2 Preheat the oven to 400°F. Put the squash on a baking sheet and bake 30 minutes until the flesh is soft enough to scoop out. (9-12) Meanwhile, mix the toasted pine nuts, goat cheese, fennel, leek, garlic, parsley, thyme, 2 tablespoons of the oil and ½ teaspoon of the salt in a large bowl. (6-9) Remove the squash from the oven, scoop the flesh out with a spoon, leaving a ½ inch shell, and coarsely chop the flesh. Add to the toasted pine nut mixture and mix well.

3 Spoon the mixture into the squash halves and return them to the baking sheet. Put any remaining filling in a small baking dish. Bake 30 to 35 minutes until the top of the squash is beginning to brown and the vegetables are soft.

4 Meanwhile, cook the pasta in plenty of boiling water, according to the package directions. Drain the pasta and put it in a large bowl, then mix in the remaining salt and oil. Add the extra cooked filling to the pasta and mix well. Serve hot with the stuffed squash and avocado salad.

(6-9)

**BAKED SQUASH, AVOCADO &
PASTA PUREE**
Put 2 tablespoons of the squash flesh and 1 tablespoon water in a ramekin and bake as above 30 minutes until completely soft. Transfer to a blender and add 2 tablespoons of chopped, cooked pasta (without the salt and oil), 2 tablespoons of avocado and 3 tablespoons water. Blend 30 seconds, adding extra water 1 teaspoon at a time, until smooth. Serve warm.

(9-12)

PASTA WITH BAKED SQUASH, AVOCADO & VEG
Put 1 tablespoon of the squash flesh, 2 fennel pieces, 1 tablespoon of the leek and 1 tablespoon water in a ramekin and bake as above 30 minutes until the vegetables are completely soft. Transfer to a blender and add 2 tablespoons of chopped, cooked pasta (without the salt and oil), 2 tablespoons of avocado and 3 tablespoons water. Pulse 15 seconds, adding extra water 1 teaspoon at a time, until the mixture forms a lumpy puree. Serve warm.

When you're running out of steam, here is a great recipe to throw together. You can make this casserole with kale instead of spinach. Quickly put it together, then snuggle on the couch with your family while it quietly bakes in the oven.

Spinach & Ricotta Pasta Casserole

SERVES: 2 adults, 1 child and 1 baby
PREPARATION TIME: 15 minutes
COOKING TIME: 35 minutes
STORAGE: Refrigerate up to 3 days.

....

10½ ounces brown rice pasta, millet pasta, quinoa pasta or buckwheat pasta, any shape
2 tablespoons unsalted butter, plus extra for greasing
1 onion, finely chopped
9 ounces fresh or defrosted, frozen baby spinach leaves, finely chopped
8 ounces ricotta cheese
1 teaspoon chopped rosemary leaves
½ teaspoon finely chopped thyme leaves
4 tablespoons extra virgin olive oil
1¼ teaspoons fine sea salt
10½ ounces drained, bottled or canned artichoke hearts in water or oil, chopped

1 Preheat the oven to 350°F and grease a large baking dish with butter. Cook the pasta in plenty of boiling water for half the time directed by the package directions. **(6-9)** **(9-12)** Drain well and set aside.

2 Meanwhile, heat the butter in a large, heavy-bottomed skillet over medium heat until melted. Add the onion and cook, stirring occasionally, 5 minutes until beginning to brown. Remove from the heat and mix in the pasta, spinach, ricotta, rosemary, thyme, oil, salt and 1¼ cups water and stir until well combined and the ricotta has melted.

3 Arrange the artichokes over the bottom of the baking dish, cover with the spinach and pasta mixture and smooth the surface with a spatula. Bake 30 minutes until bubbling and beginning to brown. Serve hot.

(6-9) ARTICHOKE & PASTA PUREE
Leave 3 tablespoons of the cooked pasta to cook for the full time recommended by the package directions. Drain well and chop. Transfer to a blender and add 6 artichoke pieces and 3 tablespoons water. Blend 30 seconds, adding extra water 1 teaspoon at a time, until smooth. Mix in 1 teaspoon of the oil and serve warm.

(9-12) BUTTER-FRIED ARTICHOKE PASTA
Leave 3 tablespoons of the cooked pasta to cook for the full time recommended by the package directions. Drain well and chop. Heat 1 teaspoon of the butter in a heavy-bottomed skillet until melted. Add the pasta, 6 artichoke pieces and 1 teaspoon of the onion and cook 10 minutes until completely soft. Transfer to a blender and add 3 tablespoons water. Pulse 15 seconds, adding extra water 1 teaspoon at a time, until the mixture forms a lumpy puree. Serve warm.

Here is my new love instead of risotto. The flavors are absolutely wonderful and I don't have to stand over the hob. Peas, which are often a favorite with children because they are a great finger food, are sweet and packed with nutrients like antioxidants.

Baked Lemon & Pea Rice

SERVES: 2 adults, 1 child and 1 baby
PREPARATION TIME: 20 minutes, plus at least 7 hours soaking
COOKING TIME: 45 minutes
STORAGE: Refrigerate up to 3 days.

....

heaped 1 cup brown Arborio or risotto rice
1 tablespoon plain yogurt or kefir, for soaking
4 tablespoons extra virgin olive oil
1 leek, quartered lengthwise and sliced
zest of 1 lemon
generous 2 cups vegetable stock
heaped ¾ cup defrosted, frozen peas or fresh, podded peas
4 tablespoons chopped parsley leaves
1¾ ounces Parmesan cheese, grated
2 tablespoons lemon juice

1 Put the rice and yogurt in a large bowl and cover generously with warm water. Let soak, covered, 7 hours or overnight at room temperature. Drain well. (6-9) (9-12)

2 Preheat the oven to 400°F. Pour the oil into a large casserole dish and heat a large saucepan over medium-high heat until hot. Add the soaked rice to the pan and cook, stirring continuously, 5 minutes, or until dry. Transfer the rice to the casserole dish and stir well, making sure the rice is thoroughly coated in the oil. Mix in the leek and ¾ of the lemon zest, then pour in the stock and stir well. Bake 35 to 40 minutes until the rice is soft but still has a slight bite and there is only a little stock left in the casserole dish.

3 Remove the casserole dish from the oven and stir in the peas, 3 tablespoons of the parsley, ¾ of the Parmesan and the lemon juice. Serve warm, sprinkled with the remaining lemon zest, parsley and Parmesan.

(6-9) ARBORIO RICE & PEA PUREE
Put 4 tablespoons of the soaked rice in a saucepan, add generous 1½ cups boiling water and simmer, covered, over low heat 50 minutes. Add 2 tablespoons of the peas and simmer, covered, 10 minutes longer until completely soft. Transfer to a blender and add 3 tablespoons water. Blend 30 seconds, adding extra water 1 teaspoon at a time, until smooth. Mix in 1 teaspoon of the oil and serve warm.

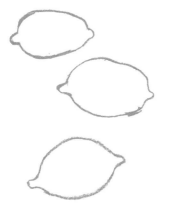

(9-12) ARBORIO RICE WITH PEAS, LEEKS & PARSLEY
Put 4 tablespoons of the soaked rice in a saucepan, add generous 1½ cups boiling water and simmer, covered, over low heat 50 minutes. Add 2 tablespoons of the peas, 1 tablespoon of the leek and 1 teaspoon of the parsley and simmer, covered, 10 minutes longer until completely soft. Transfer to a blender and add 3 tablespoons water. Blend 15 seconds, adding extra water 1 teaspoon at a time, until the mixture forms a lumpy puree. Mix in 1 teaspoon of the oil and serve warm.

Stuffing is a good way to introduce grains other than rice into your cooking and your kids. Just scoop the raw zucchini out and fill with this crunchy, tasty mix of millet, Parmesan and seeds roasted in tamari.

Zucchini Baked with Toasted Seeds

SERVES: 2 adults, 1 child and 1 baby
PREPARATION TIME: 25 minutes, plus at least 7 hours soaking and 20 minutes cooking the millet
COOKING TIME: 30 minutes
STORAGE: Refrigerate up to 3 days.

....

¼ ounce arame (optional)
2 tablespoons sunflower seeds
2 tablespoons pumpkin seeds
1 tablespoon sesame seeds
1 teaspoon tamari soy sauce or shoyu soy sauce
a large pinch of cayenne pepper
4 zucchini, halved
1 extra-large egg
1 tablespoon extra virgin olive oil, plus extra for greasing
½ recipe quantity cooked millet, cooked quinoa or cooked brown rice (see page 22)
2½ tablespoons plain yogurt
1 ounce Parmesan cheese, grated
½ teaspoon fine sea salt

1 Preheat the oven to 400°F and grease a large baking dish with oil. Using your fingertips, crush the arame in a small bowl, if using. Add 4 tablespoons boiling water and let soak 10 minutes. Mix together the seeds, tamari and cayenne pepper in a small bowl.

2 Scoop the flesh out of the zucchini halves with a spoon leaving a ½-inch shell, then coarsely chop the flesh. (6-9) (9-12) Discard the flesh. In a large bowl, lightly beat the egg with a whisk. Add the arame, if using, oil, cooked millet, yogurt, Parmesan and salt and mix well. Spoon the mixture evenly into the hollowed out zucchini halves and sprinkle the seed mix on top. Put the zucchini halves in the baking dish and bake 30 minutes until the zucchini are just soft and the topping is browned. Serve hot.

(6-9) **MILLET & ZUCCHINI PUREE**
Put 4 tablespoons of the cooked millet and generous ½ cup boiling water in a saucepan and simmer, covered, over low heat 20 minutes until completely soft. Put 3 tablespoons of the zucchini flesh in a steamer and steam, covered, 10 minutes until completely soft. Transfer to a blender and add the cooked millet and 3 tablespoons water. Blend 30 seconds, adding extra water 1 teaspoon at a time, until smooth. Mix in 1 teaspoon of the oil and serve warm.

(9-12) **MILLET & ZUCCHINI WITH YOGURT**
Put 4 tablespoons of the cooked millet and generous ½ cup boiling water in a saucepan and simmer, covered, over low heat 20 minutes until completely soft. Put 3 tablespoons of the zucchini flesh in a steamer and steam, covered, 10 minutes until completely soft. Transfer to a blender and add the cooked millet, 2 tablespoons of the yogurt and 2 tablespoons water. Pulse 15 seconds, adding extra water 1 teaspoon at a time, until the mixture forms a lumpy puree. Serve warm.

This is so creamy with the melting feta. Everything comes together so much that you can't even tell that it's millet. I find casseroles are another easy way to try a grain other than rice or pasta.

Millet & Mung Bean Casserole

SERVES: 2 adults, 1 child and 1 baby
PREPARATION TIME: 30 minutes, plus at least 12 hours soaking and 55 minutes cooking the mung beans (optional), plus at least 7 hours soaking and 20 minutes cooking the millet
COOKING TIME: 30 minutes
STORAGE: Refrigerate up to 3 days.

....

4 tablespoons extra virgin olive oil, plus extra for greasing
3½ ounces broccoli, cut into bite-size florets
⅔ cup defrosted, frozen peas or fresh, podded peas
1 leek, halved lengthwise and sliced
7 ounces feta cheese, diced
2 tablespoons Worcestershire sauce
1 teaspoon fine sea salt
1 recipe quantity cooked mung beans (see page 24) or 2 cups drained and rinsed canned mung beans
1 recipe quantity cooked millet (see page 22)
3 tablespoons unsalted butter
scant ⅔ cup dried wholegrain breadcrumbs
salad, to serve

1 Preheat the oven to 400°F and grease a large baking dish with oil. (6-9) (9-12) In a large bowl, mix together the oil, broccoli, peas, leek, feta, Worcestershire sauce, salt and ½ cup water. Add the cooked mung beans and cooked millet and mix well. (Chop and add the kombu, if used during cooking.) Put the mixture in the baking dish and smooth the top with the back of a wooden spoon.

2 Heat the butter in a saucepan over low heat until melted, then remove from the heat. Add the breadcrumbs and mix until well combined. Sprinkle the buttered breadcrumbs over the top of the millet and mung bean mixture and bake 25 to 30 minutes until bubbling and lightly browned. Serve hot with salad.

(6-9) MILLET, MUNG BEAN, BROCCOLI & PEA PUREE
Finely chop 3 broccoli pieces. Put the broccoli, 2 tablespoons of the cooked millet, 1 tablespoon of the cooked mung beans, 1 tablespoon of the peas and 3 tablespoons water in a ramekin. Bake as above 20 minutes until the vegetables are completely soft. Transfer to a blender and blend 30 seconds, adding water 1 teaspoon at a time, until smooth. Mix in 1 teaspoon of the oil and serve warm.

(9-12) MILLET, MUNG BEAN, BROCCOLI, PEA & LEEK CASSEROLE
Finely chop 3 broccoli pieces and 1 teaspoon of the leek. Put the broccoli and leek, 2 tablespoons of the cooked millet, 1 tablespoon of the cooked mung beans, 1 tablespoon of the peas and 3 tablespoons water in a ramekin. Bake as above 20 minutes until the vegetables are completely soft. Transfer to a blender and pulse 15 seconds, adding extra water 1 teaspoon at a time, until the mixture forms a lumpy puree. Mix in 1 teaspoon of the oil and serve warm.

I love the idea of lasagne, but I'm not keen on a white sauce and didn't want to have to make tomato sauce because lasagne already takes a lot of time. Here is the first recipe I created for this book, with the help of my friend Anita. We gathered some of my favorite ingredients and put together this amazing dish.

Roasted Vegetable Lasagne

SERVES: 4 adults and 4 children
PREPARATION TIME: 1 hour
COOKING TIME: 1 hour 10 minutes
STORAGE: Refrigerate up to 3 days.

....

2 pounds 4 ounces plum tomatoes, thickly sliced
generous ½ cup olive oil, plus extra for greasing
3 tablespoons chopped parsley leaves
1 tablespoon chopped oregano leaves or 1 teaspoon dried oregano
1 tablespoon finely chopped thyme leaves or 1 teaspoon dried thyme
10½ ounces drained, bottled or canned artichoke hearts in water or oil, thinly sliced lengthwise
1 small yellow bell pepper, halved, seeded and thinly sliced
2 red onions, halved and thinly sliced
1 small zucchini, thinly sliced
1 teaspoon salt
9 wholegrain spelt lasagne sheets or wholewheat lasagne sheets
1 pound 2 ounces mozzarella balls, drained and thinly sliced
scant ¾ cup drained capers in salt or brine, rinsed
5½ ounces drained, bottled or canned pitted black olives, chopped
4 garlic cloves, thinly sliced
2 ounces Parmesan cheese, grated
avocado salad, to serve

1 Preheat the oven to 500°F and grease one baking dish and one large baking dish with oil. Put the tomatoes in the baking dish and drizzle 3 tablespoons of the oil over the top. Sprinkle with the parsley, oregano and thyme and toss gently but thoroughly. Put the artichokes, bell pepper, onions and zucchini in the large baking dish, drizzle with 5 tablespoons of the oil and toss gently. Put both baking dishes in the oven and bake 30 minutes until the vegetables are soft and beginning to brown. Remove from the oven and set aside to cool. (6-9) (9-12)

2 Turn the oven down to 400°F. Transfer the roasted vegetables in the large baking dish to a bowl, add the salt and toss well.

3 Drizzle the remaining oil over the bottom of the large baking dish, then spread ⅓ of the roasted tomatoes evenly over the bottom, followed by 3 lasagne sheets, ¼ of the mozzarella, ⅓ of the roasted vegetable mixture, ⅓ of the capers, ¼ of the olives and ⅓ of the garlic. Repeat the layers twice, then sprinkle the Parmesan and the remaining mozzarella and olives evenly over the top.

4 Bake 40 minutes until the top is bubbling and golden brown. Serve hot with avocado salad.

6-9 ARTICHOKE, ZUCCHINI & AVOCADO PUREE
Put 3 tablespoons of the roasted artichokes, 2 tablespoons of the roasted zucchini, 2 tablespoons of avocado and 3 tablespoons water in a blender. Blend 30 seconds, adding extra water 1 teaspoon at a time, until smooth. Serve warm.

9-12 ROASTED ARTICHOKE, ZUCCHINI, ONION & AVOCADO
Put 2 tablespoons each of the roasted artichokes, zucchini, onions and avocado and 3 tablespoons water in a blender. Pulse 15 seconds, adding extra water 1 teaspoon at a time, until the mixture forms a lumpy puree. Serve warm.

Teriyaki Tofu

MAKES: 12 skewers
PREPARATION TIME: 50 minutes,
plus 1 hour marinating, plus at least
7 hours soaking and 40 minutes
cooking the red Camargue rice
COOKING TIME: 25 minutes
STORAGE: Refrigerate up to 3 days.

....

6 tablespoons extra virgin olive oil
6 ounces tofu or tempeh, cut into
    24 bite-size pieces
1 small red bell pepper, halved, seeded
    and cut into 12 pieces
12 button mushrooms
1 zucchini, cut into 12 slices
1 small fennel bulb, cut into 12 pieces
3 shallots, quartered
1 teaspoon fine sea salt
1 recipe quantity cooked red Camargue
    rice or cooked brown rice
    (see page 23)

FOR THE MARINADE
1½ tablespoons cornstarch, ground
    arrowroot or crushed kuzu
1½ tablespoons tamari soy sauce or
    shoyu soy sauce
4 tablespoons mirin
1 tablespoon grated ginger root

1 Grease a shallow baking dish with 1 tablespoon of the oil. To make the marinade, mix the cornstarch and 1½ tablespoons cold water together to make a smooth paste in a bowl. Put the cornstarch mixture, generous 1⅓ cups water and all of the remaining ingredients for the marinade in a saucepan. Cook over medium heat 3 to 5 minutes, stirring continuously, until the marinade thickens. Remove the pan from the heat and set aside to cool 10 minutes. Add a little water if the marinade becomes too thick to pour.

2 (6-9) (9-12) Thread 1 piece of the tofu, 1 piece of bell pepper, a mushroom and 1 piece each of the zucchini, fennel and shallots onto a metal or bamboo skewer. Finish with another piece of the tofu and repeat with the remaining skewers. Put the skewers in the baking dish and spoon the marinade over the top. Let stand to marinate, covered, 1 hour at room temperature.

3 Preheat the broiler to medium-high. Reserve the marinade and broil the skewers 20 minutes, turning once and brushing with more of the marinade, until the vegetables and tofu are beginning to brown. Mix the salt, the remaining marinade and the remaining oil into the cooked red Camargue rice and serve warm with the skewers.

 RED RICE & ZUCCHINI PUREE
Put 4 tablespoons of the cooked red Camargue rice and generous ½ cup boiling water in a saucepan and simmer, covered, over low heat 10 minutes. Add 6 zucchini pieces and simmer, covered, 10 minutes longer until completely soft. Transfer to a blender and add 3 tablespoons water. Blend 30 seconds, adding extra water 1 teaspoon at a time, until smooth. Mix in 1 teaspoon of the oil and serve warm.

(9-12) RED RICE WITH ZUCCHINI & FENNEL
Put 4 tablespoons of the cooked red Camargue rice and generous ½ cup boiling water in a saucepan and simmer, covered, over low heat 10 minutes. Add 3 pieces each of the zucchini and fennel and simmer, covered, 10 minutes longer until completely soft. Transfer to a blender and add 3 tablespoons water. Pulse 15 seconds, adding extra water 1 teaspoon at a time, until the mixture forms a lumpy puree. Mix in 1 teaspoon of the oil and serve warm.

Hand rolls are the easiest way to eat sushi because even children can roll them, hold them and eat them. You can pile the ingredients onto the table and let everyone make their own—beautiful triangles bursting with color and flavor.

Nori Hand Rolls

MAKES: 20
PREPARATION TIME: 20 minutes, plus at least 7 hours soaking and 40 minutes cooking the brown sushi rice
COOKING TIME: 5 minutes
STORAGE: Refrigerate up to 3 days.

....

10 asparagus, woody ends removed, and halved
40 green beans, trimmed
1 teaspoon fine sea salt
1 recipe quantity cooked brown sushi rice or brown short-grain rice (see page 23)
10 nori sheets, halved lengthwise
½ tablespoon wasabi (optional)
1 beet, grated
1¼ ounces sprouts such as alfalfa, broccoli or mung (optional)

FOR THE SAUCE
2 avocados, peeled, pitted and mashed
2 tablespoons mayonnaise

1 (6-9) (9-12) Put the asparagus and green beans in a steamer and steam, covered, 5 minutes until the vegetables are cooked but still slightly crunchy. Add the salt to the cooked brown sushi rice and mix well.

2 To make the sauce, mix together the avocados and mayonnaise in a bowl until smooth.

3 To make a hand roll, spread 1 tablespoon of the sauce diagonally down the centre of 1 nori sheet, then add a little wasabi on top, if using. Put 1 tablespoon of the cooked brown sushi rice, 1 piece of asparagus, 2 green beans and 1 tablespoon each of the beet and sprouts, if using, on top of the sauce. Take the nori sheet in your hand and roll into a cone shape. Repeat with the remaining ingredients and serve.

(6-9) **GREEN BEAN, AVOCADO & RICE PUREE**
Put 4 tablespoons of the cooked brown sushi rice and generous ½ cup boiling water in a saucepan and simmer, covered, over low heat 10 minutes. Add 4 green beans and cook, covered, 10 minutes longer until completely soft. Transfer to a blender and add 2 tablespoons of the avocado and 3 tablespoons water. Blend 30 seconds, adding extra water 1 teaspoon at a time, until smooth. Serve warm.

 VEGETABLES, AVOCADO, SPROUTS, BEET & RICE
Put 4 tablespoons of the cooked brown sushi rice and generous ½ cup boiling water in a saucepan and simmer, covered, over low heat 10 minutes. Add 2 green beans and 1 asparagus piece and cook 10 minutes longer until completely soft. Transfer to a blender and add 2 tablespoons of the avocado, 1 tablespoon each of the beet and sprouts, if using, and 3 tablespoons water. Pulse 15 seconds, adding extra water 1 teaspoon at a time, until the mixture forms a lumpy puree. Serve warm.

Cheesy Loaf with Mole

SERVES: 4 adults and 4 children
PREPARATION TIME: 1 hour, plus at least 7 hours soaking and 20 minutes cooking the red quinoa, plus at least 7 hours soaking and 40 minutes cooking the red Camargue rice
COOKING TIME: 1 hour 20 minutes
STORAGE: Refrigerate up to 1 day.

....

unsalted butter, for greasing
¾ ounce dried porcini mushrooms
1 cup pecans
1 cup walnuts
5 extra-large eggs
1 onion, finely chopped
2 garlic cloves, crushed
4 tablespoons chopped parsley leaves
2 teaspoons finely chopped thyme leaves
1 teaspoon finely chopped sage leaves
½ teaspoon fine sea salt
9 ounces ricotta cheese
9 ounces cheddar cheese, grated
½ recipe quantity cooked red quinoa or quinoa (see page 22)
½ recipe quantity cooked red Camargue rice or cooked brown rice (see page 23)
avocado, cucumber and tomato salad, to serve
mayonnaise, to serve

FOR THE MOLE
2 teaspoons extra virgin olive oil
1 small onion, finely chopped
1 tablespoon cocoa powder
1 teaspoon ground cumin
1 teaspoon ground cilantro
1 garlic clove, finely chopped
5 dried Thai chilies, finely chopped
10 ounces tomatoes, diced
¼ teaspoon fine sea salt

1 Preheat the broiler to medium and grease a 9 x 5-inch loaf pan with butter. Line the loaf pan with parchment paper and grease again. Soak the porcini mushrooms in scant 1¼ cups water 20 minutes until softened. Drain, squeeze out any excess water and chop. Put the nuts on a baking sheet and broil 1 to 2 minutes until lightly browned. Remove from the broiler and roughly chop the nuts.

2 Preheat the oven to 375°F. In a large bowl, lightly beat the eggs together with a whisk. (6-9) (9-18) Add the onion, garlic, parsley, thyme, sage, salt, ricotta, cheddar, porcini mushrooms, toasted nuts, cooked red quinoa and cooked red Camargue rice and mix well. Spoon the mixture into the loaf pan, smooth the surface with the back of a metal spoon and bake 1 hour 15 minutes until risen, browned and cracked.

3 Meanwhile, make the mole. Heat the oil in a heavy-bottomed skillet over medium heat. Add the onion and cook 5 minutes until soft. Mix in all of the remaining ingredients and bring to a boil over high heat, then turn the heat down to low and simmer, covered, 15 minutes, stirring occasionally, until the vegetables are soft. Remove the loaf from the oven and let stand to cool in the pan 10 minutes. Turn the loaf out of the pan, then transfer to a serving plate, right-side up. Serve hot with the mole (for adults), and an avocado, cucumber and tomato salad with mayonnaise.

(6-9) RED RICE, RED QUINOA & AVOCADO PUREE
Put 2 tablespoons of the cooked red Camargue rice, 2 tablespoons of the cooked red quinoa and generous ½ cup boiling water in a saucepan and simmer, covered, 20 minutes until completely soft. Transfer to a blender and add 6 avocado pieces and 3 tablespoons water. Blend 30 seconds, adding extra water 1 teaspoon at a time, until smooth. Serve warm.

(9-12) RED RICE & RED QUINOA WITH AVOCADO, ONION & PARSLEY
Put 2 tablespoons of the cooked red Camargue rice, 2 tablespoons of the cooked red quinoa, 1 teaspoon each of the onion and parsley and generous ½ cup boiling water in a saucepan and simmer, covered, 20 minutes until completely soft. Transfer to a blender and add 6 avocado pieces and 3 tablespoons water. Pulse 15 seconds, adding extra water 1 teaspoon at a time, until the mixture forms a lumpy puree. Serve warm.

White food is generally so unhealthy that I decided to try to make white food that is actually good for you. I took everything white I had in the kitchen and made this soup.

White Vegetable Soup

SERVES: 4 adults and 4 children
PREPARATION TIME: 25 minutes, plus at least 12 hours soaking and 1 hour 40 minutes cooking the navy beans (optional)
COOKING TIME: 40 minutes
STORAGE: Refrigerate up to 3 days, or freeze up to 3 months.

....

2 tablespoons extra virgin olive oil, plus extra to serve
1 onion, chopped
5 garlic cloves, quartered
4 medium potatoes, chopped
½ recipe quantity cooked dried navy beans (see page 24) or 1 cup drained and rinsed canned navy beans
2 cups small cauliflower florets
½ tablespoon fine sea salt
hot pepper sauce, to serve
salad, to serve
wholegrain bread, to serve

1 Heat the oil in a large, heavy-bottomed saucepan over medium heat. Add the onion and cook, stirring occasionally, 5 minutes until beginning to brown, then turn the heat up to high. Add the garlic, potatoes and 2 cups water. Bring to a simmer and cook, covered, over low heat 20 minutes longer. Add the cooked navy beans and cauliflower and cook 10 minutes longer until the cauliflower is soft. (Chop and add the kombu, if used during cooking.) Stir in the salt and remove the pan from the heat.

2 Transfer ½ of the soup to a blender and blend until creamy. Return the blended soup to the pan, reheating if necessary. Serve hot, drizzled with hot pepper sauce, and with salad, wholegrain bread and oil.

6-9 NAVY BEANS & CAULIFLOWER PUREE
Put 6 cauliflower pieces in a steamer and steam, covered, 10 minutes until completely soft. Transfer to a blender and add 3 tablespoons of the cooked navy beans and 3 tablespoons water. Blend 30 seconds, adding extra water 1 teaspoon at a time, until smooth. Mix in 1 teaspoon of the oil and serve warm.

9-12 NAVY BEANS, CAULIFLOWER & GARLIC
Put 6 cauliflower pieces and 1 garlic piece in a steamer and steam, covered, 10 minutes until completely soft. Transfer to a blender and add 3 tablespoons of the cooked navy beans and 3 tablespoons water. Pulse 15 seconds, adding extra water 1 teaspoon at a time, until the mixture forms a lumpy puree. Mix in 1 teaspoon of the oil and serve warm.

This is a simple dinner, but it has great flavors. Toasted sesame seeds, miso, ginger and a hint of chili make a mouthwatering mix. The water chestnuts add crunchy texture to the soft noodles and there is plenty of sauce to go around.

Spicy Soba with Bok Choy

SERVES: 2 adults, 1 child and 1 baby
PREPARATION TIME: 30 minutes
COOKING TIME: 15 minutes
STORAGE: Refrigerate up to 3 days.

....

10½ ounces 100 percent buckwheat soba noodles or brown rice noodles
2 tablespoons sesame seeds
5 tablespoons white miso
5 tablespoons mirin
1 tablespoon finely chopped ginger root
4 tablespoons sesame oil
3 scallions, white parts finely chopped and green parts cut into rings
7 ounces bok choy, coarsely chopped
5½ ounces broccoli, cut into bite-size pieces
3½ ounces water chestnuts, halved
a large pinch of crushed chili

1 Cook the noodles in plenty of boiling water, according to the package directions. Gradually add the noodles to the pan to keep the water at boiling point. Stir gently to prevent the noodles from sticking to the bottom of the pan. Drain, then rinse the noodles under cold running water to prevent further cooking and to make sure the noodles don't stick together. Drain again.

2 Meanwhile, heat a large skillet over medium heat until hot. Add the sesame seeds and dry-fry 3 to 4 minutes until beginning to brown. Remove from the heat and set aside. Mix the white miso, mirin and ginger in a bowl.

3 Heat the oil in a wok or large skillet over medium-high heat. Add the white part of the scallions and stir-fry 2 minutes. Add the bok choy, broccoli and ¾ cup water and cook 5 to 7 minutes until just tender. Remove from the heat, then stir in the toasted sesame seeds, white miso mixture, water chestnuts and crushed chili. Serve hot with the noodles and the green part of the scallions sprinkled over the top.

6-9 BUCKWHEAT NOODLE & BROCCOLI PUREE
Heat 1 teaspoon of the oil and 3 tablespoons water in a skillet. Add 6 broccoli pieces and cook, covered, over low heat 10 minutes until completely soft. Transfer to a blender and add 3 tablespoons of chopped, cooked noodles and 3 tablespoons water. Blend 30 seconds, adding extra water 1 teaspoon at a time, until smooth. Serve warm.

 BUCKWHEAT NOODLES, BOK CHOY, BROCCOLI & SCALLION
Heat 1 teaspoon of the oil and 3 tablespoons water in a skillet. Add 1 tablespoon of the bok choy, 6 broccoli pieces and 1 teaspoon of the white part of the scallions and cook, covered, over low heat 10 minutes until completely soft. Transfer to a blender and add 3 tablespoons of chopped, cooked noodles and 3 tablespoons water. Pulse 15 seconds, adding extra water 1 teaspoon at a time, until the mixture forms a lumpy puree. Serve warm.

chapter four
baked treats

We finish off with the absolute joy of baking.
Here are breakfast breads, healthy snacks, slices
and cakes, pies and desserts—and fruits galore.
Not a huge fan of dessert, I make my sweet
treats with ingredients like wholewheat flour, rice
malt syrup, fruits or vegetables. But you'd never
know it—guests never guess that my brownies
contain sweet potatoes and who cares if pie is
made with wholewheat pastry?

This chapter is not about serving desserts
to your children every day—and certainly not to
a baby. But it will provide you with methods for
cooking and baking fruits, like Apple & Blueberry
Squares, which are great for snacking or adding
to lunch bags, and means you've got Baked Apple
& Buckwheat Puree for a 6 to 9 month old or
Baked Apple & Blueberry for a 9 to 12 month old.

Breakfast Bread

MAKES: 1 loaf (about 16 slices)
PREPARATION TIME: 20 minutes, plus at least 3 hours rising
COOKING TIME: 35 minutes
STORAGE: Store in an airtight container up to 2 days, then refrigerate up to 3 days or slice and freeze up to 3 months.

....

3 cups wholegrain spelt flour or wholewheat flour, plus extra for dusting
1 cup rolled oats or any flaked wholegrain, such as millet, barley or buckwheat
⅔ cup dried unsulphured apricots, ¾ halved and ¼ finely chopped
3 tablespoons sunflower seeds
3 tablespoons flaxseeds
2 tablespoons sesame seeds
2 teaspoons fine sea salt
2 teaspoons active dry yeast
4 tablespoons rice malt syrup or 3 tablespoons cane sugar
2 tablespoons sunflower oil, plus extra for greasing
2½ tablespoons plain yogurt
unsalted butter, for greasing and to serve

1 (6-9) (9-12) Mix the flour, oats, apricots, seeds and salt in a large bowl. Make a well in the center of the mixture and add the yeast and rice malt syrup. Pour in scant 1 cup warm water to dissolve the yeast and rice malt syrup.

2 Add the oil and yogurt and bring the dough together with a wooden spoon. Turn the dough out onto a work surface and knead 10 minutes until smooth and elastic, adding a little more flour if the dough sticks to your hands or work surface. Rinse and dry the mixing bowl, then lightly grease it with oil. Return the dough to the mixing bowl and turn until completely coated in oil. Let rise 1½ to 2 hours until doubled in size.

3 Grease a 9 x 5-inch loaf pan with butter. Turn the dough out onto a work surface and punch it down to get rid of any air bubbles. Knead 1 minute, then shape into a log the length of the pan. Put the dough in the pan and let rise 1½ to 2 hours longer until doubled in size.

4 Preheat the oven to 425°F. Bake 15 minutes, then turn the heat down to 375°F and bake 20 minutes longer until firm to the touch. Remove from the oven and let cool 15 minutes, then turn out of the loaf pan, transfer to a cooling rack and let cool. Serve warm or toasted with butter.

 APRICOT PUREE
Put 8 apricot halves and scant ⅔ cup water in a saucepan. Bring to a boil over high heat, then turn the heat down to low and simmer, covered, 15 minutes until completely soft. Let cool slightly, then transfer to a blender and blend 30 seconds, adding water 1 teaspoon at a time, until smooth. Serve warm.

 APRICOT & OAT MIX
Put 8 apricot halves, 4 tablespoons of the oats, ½ tablespoon of the yogurt and 1 cup water in a saucepan. Let soak, covered, 7 hours or overnight at room temperature. Bring to a boil over high heat, then turn the heat down to low and simmer, covered, 15 minutes, stirring occasionally, until completely soft. Transfer to a blender and pulse 15 seconds, adding water 1 teaspoon at a time, until the mixture forms a lumpy puree. Serve warm.

Banana bread is a great way to use up old bananas. Made with wholegrain flour and walnuts, this has evolved from my mom's recipe from when we were kids. I remember waiting with my sisters and brother to lick the bowl and spatula.

Banana Walnut Bread

MAKES: 1 loaf (about 16 slices)
PREPARATION TIME: 30 minutes
COOKING TIME: 1 hour
STORAGE: Store in an airtight container up to 2 days, then refrigerate up to 3 days or slice and freeze up to 3 months.

·····································

1 cup wholegrain spelt flour or wholewheat flour
1 cup white spelt flour or all-purpose flour, plus extra for dusting
2 teaspoons baking powder
½ teaspoon fine sea salt
½ cup (1 stick) plus 1 tablespoon unsalted butter, at room temperature, plus extra for greasing and to serve
¾ cup cane sugar
2 extra-large eggs
½ cup oat milk, rice milk or water
1 teaspoon vanilla extract
2 ripe or overripe bananas, mashed
½ cup walnuts, chopped

1 Preheat the oven to 350°F and grease and flour a 9 x 5-inch loaf pan.

2 Mix the flours, baking powder and salt in a bowl. Put the butter and sugar in a large mixing bowl and beat, using an electric mixer, 5 minutes until creamy. Add the eggs, one at a time, beating well after each addition. (6-9) (9-12) Add the oat milk, vanilla extract, bananas, walnuts and the flour mixture and beat 30 seconds until just combined, but take care not to overmix.

3 Pour the mixture into the loaf pan and level the surface, using a clean knife. Bake 55 minutes to 1 hour until firm to the touch, browned and a toothpick inserted into the center comes out clean. Remove from the oven and let cool 20 minutes. Run a knife around the edge of the loaf, then turn out of the pan, transfer to a cooling rack and let cool. Serve warm or at room temperature, plain or with butter.

(6-9) **BANANA PUREE**
Put ¼ of the mashed banana and 2 tablespoons water in a blender. Blend 30 seconds, adding extra water 1 teaspoon at a time, until smooth. Serve warm or at room temperature.

(9-12) **BANANA & OAT MILK MIX**
Put ¼ of the mashed banana and 2 tablespoons of the oat milk in a bowl and mix until well combined. Serve warm or at room temperature.

Corn bread makes a tasty change from flour-based snacks and is good warm or cold, plain or toasted with butter. Apricots add a nice touch here, providing extra sweetness and goodness. Make sure you buy organic apricots, which are unsulphured.

Apricot Corn Bread

MAKES: 1 loaf (about 16 slices)
PREPARATION TIME: 25 minutes
COOKING TIME: 1 hour and 5 minutes
STORAGE: Store in airtight container up to 2 days, then refrigerate up to 3 days.

....

scant 2¼ cups cornmeal or instant polenta
1 cup white spelt flour or all-purpose flour
½ cup brown rice flour
heaped 1 cup cane sugar
2 teaspoons baking soda
1 teaspoon fine sea salt
4½ tablespoons unsalted butter or 4 tablespoons sunflower oil, plus extra for greasing
2 extra-large eggs
1 cup plain yogurt
heaped ¾ cup dried, unsulphured apricots, finely chopped

1 Preheat the oven to 325°F. Grease a 9 x 5-inch loaf pan with butter and line with parchment paper. **(6-9)** **(9-12)** In a large mixing bowl, mix together the cornmeal, flours, sugar, baking soda and salt. Heat the butter in a saucepan over low heat until melted, then remove from the heat. In another bowl, lightly beat the eggs together with a whisk. Add the melted butter, yogurt, apricots and 1 cup water and mix well.

2 Add the egg mixture to the flour mixture and beat slowly with a wooden spoon until just combined, but be careful not to overmix. Pour the mixture into the loaf pan and level the surface, using a clean knife. Bake 1 hour until lightly browned and a toothpick inserted into the center comes out clean. Remove from the oven and let cool 15 minutes, then turn out of the pan, transfer to a cooling rack, remove the parchment paper and let cool. Serve warm.

(6-9) BAKED APRICOT PUREE
Put 2 tablespoons of the apricots, 1 tablespoon of the rice flour and 5 tablespoons water in a greased ramekin and mix well. Bake as above 15 minutes until the apricots are completely soft and the top has lightly browned. Transfer to a blender and add 3 tablespoons water. Blend 30 seconds, adding extra water 1 teaspoon at a time, until smooth. Serve warm.

(9-12) CORNMEAL APRICOT DESSERT
Put 2 tablespoons of the apricots, 1 tablespoon each of the rice flour and cornmeal, 2 tablespoons of the yogurt and 3 tablespoons water in a greased ramekin and mix well. Bake as above 20 minutes until the apricots are completely soft and the top has lightly browned. Transfer to a blender and pulse 15 seconds, adding water 1 teaspoon at a time, until the mixture forms a lumpy puree. Serve warm.

This is an old family favorite that my mom used
to make when I was growing up. It is loaded with
plums and heavy with oats—perfect for breakfast
or snacking. My brother David and I loved it when
we were little, and now it is a favorite with Nicholas.

Plum Oatmeal Bread

MAKES: 1 loaf (about 16 slices)
PREPARATION TIME: 20 minutes
COOKING TIME: 1 hour
STORAGE: Store in an airtight
container up to 2 days, then
refrigerate up to 3 days or slice
and freeze up to 3 months.

....

unsalted butter, for greasing
1 cup wholegrain spelt flour or
   wholewheat flour
1 cup white spelt flour or all-purpose
   flour
1 cup rolled oats
¾ cup cane sugar
1 tablespoon baking powder
1 teaspoon fine sea salt
2 extra-large eggs
1 cup oat milk, rice milk or water
4 tablespoons sunflower oil
2 teaspoons vanilla extract
10 ounces plums, pitted and chopped

1 Preheat the oven to 350°F. Grease a 9 x 5-inch loaf pan with butter,
line with parchment paper and grease again.

2 **(9-12)** In a large mixing bowl, mix together the flours, oats, sugar, baking
powder and salt. In another bowl, lightly beat the eggs together with a
whisk. Add the oat milk, oil and vanilla extract and whisk. Add the egg
mixture to the flour mixture and beat slowly with a wooden spoon until
just combined, but be careful not to overmix. **(6-9)** Using a large metal
spoon, carefully fold in the plums. Pour the mixture into the loaf pan
and level the surface, using a clean knife.

3 Bake 50 minutes to 1 hour until lightly browned and a toothpick inserted
into the center comes out clean. Remove from the oven and let cool
20 minutes. Run a knife around the edge of the loaf, then turn out of the
pan, transfer to a cooling rack, remove the parchment paper and let cool.
Serve warm or at room temperature.

(6-9) **PLUM PUREE**
Put 4 tablespoons of the plums and 2 tablespoons water in a blender.
Blend 30 seconds, adding extra water 1 teaspoon at a time, until smooth.
Serve warm or at room temperature.

(9-12) **PLUM PUDDING**
Put 4 tablespoons of the oats, 2 tablespoons of the plums and ¾ cup water
in a small baking dish. Let soak, covered, 7 hours or overnight at room
temperature. Bake as above 30 minutes until completely soft. Transfer to
a blender and add 2 tablespoons water. Pulse 15 seconds, adding extra water
1 teaspoon at a time, until the mixture forms a lumpy puree. Serve warm.

These are quick to prepare—much easier than cookies. Serve them mid-morning when your kids are home on the weekends, in their lunch bag at school or when they come in from playing.

Cinnamon Raisin Bars

MAKES: 12
PREPARATION TIME: 15 minutes
COOKING TIME: 45 minutes
STORAGE: Store in an airtight container up to 2 days, then refrigerate up to 3 days.

....

3 extra-large eggs
1 cup sunflower oil, plus extra
 for greasing
1 cup rice malt syrup or ¾ cup
 plus 2 tablespoons cane sugar
2 teaspoons vanilla extract
3 cups rolled oats
1½ cups wholegrain spelt flour or
 wholewheat flour
1¼ cup raisins
4 teaspoons ground cinnamon
1 teaspoon baking powder
1 teaspoon fine sea salt

1 Preheat the oven to 325°F and grease a 9 x 13-inch baking dish with oil. In a bowl, lightly beat the eggs together with a whisk. Mix in the oil, rice malt syrup, vanilla extract and 4 tablespoons water (or ½ cup water if using cane sugar).

2 (6-9) (9-12) In a large mixing bowl, mix together the oats, flour, raisins, cinnamon, baking powder and salt. Add the egg mixture to the flour mixture and stir well with a wooden spoon until mixed. Pour the mixture into the baking dish and smooth the surface with a spatula.

3 Bake 45 minutes until lightly browned. Remove from oven and let cool 5 minutes. Cut into squares and serve warm or at room temperature.

(6-9)

BAKED OATS PUREE
Put 4 tablespoons of the oats and ¾ cup water in a small baking dish and mix. Let soak, covered, 7 hours or overnight at room temperature. Bake as above 30 minutes until completely soft. Transfer to a blender and add 2 tablespoons water. Blend 30 seconds, adding extra water 1 teaspoon at a time, until smooth. Serve warm.

(9-12)

RAISIN PUDDING
Put 4 tablespoons of the oats, 1 tablespoon of the raisins and ¾ cup water in a small baking dish and mix. Let soak, covered, 7 hours or overnight at room temperature. Bake as above 30 minutes until completely soft. Transfer to a blender and add 2 tablespoons water. Pulse 15 seconds, adding extra water 1 teaspoon at a time, until the mixture forms a lumpy puree. Serve warm.

Most children—and mine—adore berries. I make these muffins with mashed raspberries and chopped peaches —and they can't resist them. Perfect for breakfast or as a snack, these are great for the whole family. Jessica's friend, Josie, couldn't wait to try one!

Peach & Raspberry Muffins

MAKES: 12
PREPARATION TIME: 25 minutes
COOKING TIME: 30 minutes
STORAGE: Refrigerate up to 3 days.

....

5 tablespoons unsalted butter, plus extra for greasing if needed
2 cups wholegrain spelt flour or wholewheat flour
½ cup cane sugar
2 teaspoons baking powder
½ teaspoon fine sea salt
2 extra-large eggs
scant 1 cup oat milk, rice milk or water
4½ ounces peaches, pitted and diced
⅔ cup fresh or defrosted, frozen raspberries, mashed

1 Preheat the oven to 375°F and grease a 12-cup muffin pan with butter or line with paper cupcake liners. Heat the butter in a saucepan over low heat until melted. Remove from the heat and let cool slightly. In a bowl, mix together the flour, sugar, baking powder and salt. In a large mixing bowl, lightly beat the eggs together with a whisk. Add the melted butter and oat milk and whisk. Add the flour mixture and whisk until just combined, but be careful not to overmix.

2 Using a large metal spoon, carefully fold in the peaches and raspberries. Spoon the mixture evenly into the muffin cups, filling each cup until it is nearly full. Bake 25 to 30 minutes until golden and a toothpick inserted into the center comes out clean. Remove from the oven and let cool 5 minutes, then turn out of the pan and transfer to a cooling rack. Serve warm.

 PEACH PUREE
Put 5 tablespoons of the peaches and 2 tablespoons water in a blender. Blend 30 seconds, adding extra water 1 teaspoon at a time, until smooth. Serve warm or at room temperature.

9-12 PEACH & RASPBERRY MIX
Put 4 tablespoons of the peaches, 1 tablespoon of the raspberries and 2 tablespoons water in a blender. Pulse 15 seconds, adding extra water 1 teaspoon at a time, until the mixture forms a lumpy puree. Serve warm or at room temperature.

Irresistible to children and grown-ups, these are densely chocolatey and lightly sweet. These brownies are made with sweet potato so they are a twist on the American classic. Although the rice malt syrup won't overexcite you, the chocolate will, so go easy.

Sweet Potato Brownies

MAKES: 9
PREPARATION TIME: 30 minutes
COOKING TIME: 40 minutes
STORAGE: Refrigerate up to 3 days.

....

12 ounces sweet potatoes, peeled and diced
6½ tablespoons unsalted butter, plus extra for greasing
½ cup unsweetened cocoa powder
2 teaspoons vanilla extract
2 extra-large eggs
1 cup rice malt syrup or ¾ cup cane sugar
1 cup plus 1 tablespoon wholegrain spelt flour or wholewheat flour
1½ teaspoons baking powder
½ teaspoon fine sea salt

1 Preheat the oven to 350°F. Grease an 8 x 8-inch baking pan with butter, line with parchment paper and grease again. Put the sweet potatoes in a steamer and steam, covered, 8 to 10 minutes until completely soft. ⑥-⑨ ⑨-⑫ Transfer to a large bowl and mash thoroughly until smooth.

2 Heat the butter in a saucepan over low heat until melted. Remove from the heat, add the cocoa powder and vanilla extract and stir until well combined. In a small bowl, lightly beat the eggs together with a whisk. Add the eggs, cocoa mixture and rice malt syrup to the sweet potatoes and mix well. In another bowl, mix together the flour, baking powder and salt, then add to the sweet potato mixture and fold until well mixed, but be careful not to overmix.

3 Spoon the mixture into the baking pan and smooth the surface with a spatula. Bake 35 to 40 minutes until the surface is cracked and a toothpick inserted into the center comes out clean. Remove from the oven and let cool in the pan 5 minutes. Cut into squares and transfer to a cooling rack to cool. Serve warm or at room temperature.

 SWEET POTATO PUREE
Put 5 tablespoons of the steamed sweet potato and 3 tablespoons water in a blender. Blend 30 seconds, adding extra water 1 teaspoon at a time, until smooth. Serve warm.

 BUTTERY MASHED SWEET POTATO
Put 5 tablespoons of the steamed sweet potato and 3 tablespoons water in a blender. Pulse 15 seconds, adding extra water 1 teaspoon at a time, until the mixture forms a lumpy puree. Mix with 1 teaspoon of the melted butter and serve warm.

It's hard to go wrong with lemon desserts, and after a satisfying meal, this pudding is perfect because it is light and refreshing. The drizzled mango accents the flavor beautifully and is wonderful for your baby.

Lemon Upside-Down Cake with Mango Puree

SERVES: 10
PREPARATION TIME: 20 minutes
COOKING TIME: 45 minutes
STORAGE: Refrigerate the cake and the mango puree up to 3 days.

....

⅓ cup firmly packed brown sugar
¾ cup (1½ sticks) plus ½ tablespoon softened, unsalted butter, plus extra for greasing
2 lemons, finely sliced and seeds removed
heaped 1½ cups wholegrain spelt flour or wholewheat flour
2 teaspoons baking powder
⅓ cup instant polenta
½ teaspoon fine sea salt
heaped ½ cup cane sugar
2 extra-large eggs
1 teaspoon vanilla extract
zest of 1 lemon
½ cup oat milk, rice milk or water

FOR THE MANGO PUREE
2 mangoes, peeled, pitted and chopped

1 Preheat the oven to 350°F and grease an 8-inch cake pan with butter. Put the brown sugar and 4½ tablespoons of the butter in a saucepan and heat over low heat 2 to 3 minutes, stirring continuously, until the butter has melted and the brown sugar has dissolved. Pour the mixture into the cake pan and arrange the lemons over the top (as close together as you can). Mix the flour, baking powder, polenta and salt in a large mixing bowl.

2 Using an electric mixer, beat together the cane sugar and the remaining butter in a mixing bowl 3 minutes until creamy. Beat in the eggs, one at a time, 30 seconds each until thoroughly incorporated, then beat in the vanilla extract and lemon zest. (9-12) Gradually beat in the flour mixture and the oat milk, alternating. Beat until well combined, but be careful not to overmix.

3 Pour the mixture over the lemons and smooth the surface with a spatula. Bake 35 to 40 minutes until lightly browned and a toothpick inserted into the center comes out clean. Remove from the oven and let cool 20 minutes, then turn out of the pan, transfer to a cooling rack and let cool.

4 Meanwhile, make the puree. Put the mango in a blender and blend 1 minute, adding water 1 tablespoon at a time, until smooth. (6-9) Serve the cake warm, drizzled with the puree.

 MANGO PUREE
Put 5 tablespoons of the mango puree in a bowl and serve warm or at room temperature.

 CHUNKY MANGO PUDDING
Put 5 tablespoons of the mango chunks and 1 tablespoon of the oat milk in a blender. Pulse 15 seconds, adding water 1 teaspoon at a time, until the mixture forms a lumpy puree. Serve warm or at room temperature.

This cake, which is very easy to make, is also very rich and should be enjoyed in thin slices—if you can resist the urge to go for more. It is almost like baked mousse, although the pear lightens it and adds texture.

Chocolate Pear Cake

MAKES: 1 cake
PREPARATION TIME: 25 minutes
COOKING TIME: 20 minutes
STORAGE: Store in an airtight container up to 2 days, then refrigerate up to 3 days or freeze up to 3 months.

....

1 cup (2 sticks) plus 2 tablespoons unsalted butter, softened, plus extra for greasing
3½ ounces semi-sweet chocolate, 70 percent cocoa solids, broken into small pieces
4 extra-large eggs
heaped ⅔ cup cane sugar
¼ cup plain yogurt
scant ½ cup wholegrain spelt flour or wholewheat flour
1 pear, cored and finely chopped

1 Preheat the oven to 350°F and grease an 8-inch cake pan with butter. Put the butter and chocolate in a large heatproof bowl and rest it over a saucepan of gently simmering water, making sure that the bottom of the bowl does not touch the water. Stir occasionally until the butter and chocolate have melted. Put the eggs and sugar in a bowl and beat, using an electric mixer, 10 minutes until pale and fluffy. (9-12) Mix the yogurt into the chocolate mixture to cool it a little, then add the chocolate mixture to the egg mixture and mix well. Add the flour and fold until well mixed, but be careful not to overmix.

2 Pour the mixture into the cake pan. (6-9) Spoon the pear into the pan, then push it down under the surface of the mixture with the back of the spoon. Bake 15 to 20 minutes until firm to the touch and a toothpick inserted into the center of the cake comes out clean. Remove from the oven and let cool 15 minutes, then turn out of the pan, transfer to a cooling rack and let cool. Serve warm or at room temperature.

(6-9)

PEAR PUREE
Put ½ of the pear and 2 tablespoons water in a blender. Blend 30 seconds, adding extra water 1 teaspoon at a time, until smooth. Serve warm or at room temperature.

(9-12)

PEAR & YOGURT
Put ½ of the pear, 2 tablespoons of the yogurt and 1 tablespoon water in a blender. Pulse 15 seconds, adding extra water 1 teaspoon at a time, until the mixture forms a lumpy puree. Serve warm or at room temperature.

Beautifully spiced and sweet, here's a dessert with no added sugar. The pecans on top become crunchy and provide a nice contrast to the soft, warm fruit. I made this for a girlie Sunday lunch and there wasn't a crumb left in the dish.

Baked Spiced Fruit

SERVES: 2 adults, 1 child and 1 baby
PREPARATION TIME: 25 minutes
COOKING TIME: 45 minutes
STORAGE: Refrigerate up to 3 days.

....

8 ounces peaches, pitted and chopped
1 pear, cored and chopped
⅔ cup dried unsulphured apricots, chopped
8 ounces pineapple, peeled, cored and chopped
1 cup peach juice, apricot juice or pineapple juice
2 tablespoons lemon juice
2 tablespoons wholegrain spelt flour or wholewheat flour
1 teaspoon ground cinnamon
¼ teaspoon ground cloves
1 cup pecans, halved
plain yogurt, to serve

1 Preheat the oven to 350°F. Put the peaches, pear and apricots in an 8 x 8-inch baking dish and mix well. (6-9) (9-12) Stir in the pineapple and set aside.

2 Pour the peach juice and lemon juice into a saucepan. Add the flour, cinnamon and cloves and mix together. Bring to a boil over high heat, stirring continuously. Cook 3 to 4 minutes, stirring frequently, until the sauce has thickened, then pour over the fruit. Sprinkle the pecans evenly over the top and bake 40 minutes until the fruit is bubbling and the pecans have browned. Remove from the oven and let cool in the baking dish 5 minutes. Serve warm or at room temperature with yogurt.

(6-9) BAKED PEACH, PEAR & APRICOT PUREE
Put 4 tablespoons of the peach, pear and apricot mixture and 1 tablespoon of the peach juice in a ramekin. Bake as above 15 minutes until the fruit is completely soft. Transfer to a blender and blend 30 seconds, adding water 1 teaspoon at a time, until smooth. Serve warm.

(9-12) BAKED FRUIT WITH YOGURT
Put 4 tablespoons of the peach, pear and apricot mixture and 1 tablespoon of the peach juice in a ramekin. Bake as above 15 minutes until the fruit is completely soft. Transfer to a blender and add 2 tablespoons of yogurt. Pulse 15 seconds, adding water 1 teaspoon at a time, until the mixture forms a lumpy puree. Serve warm.

Peach & Blueberry Pie

SERVES: 8
PREPARATION TIME: 45 minutes,
plus 30 minutes chilling
COOKING TIME: 50 minutes
STORAGE: Refrigerate up to 3 days.

....

FOR THE DOUGH
2 cups wholegrain spelt flour or
   wholewheat flour, plus extra
   for dusting
½ teaspoon fine sea salt
½ cup (1 stick) plus 1 tablespoon
   chilled unsalted butter, diced

FOR THE FILLING
¼ cup wholegrain spelt flour or
   wholewheat flour
1 tablespoon cornstarch, ground
   arrowroot or kuzu
⅓ cup rice malt syrup or heaped
   ¼ cup cane sugar
½ teaspoon ground nutmeg
¼ teaspoon fine sea salt
1 tablespoon lemon juice
1 teaspoon lemon zest
3 cups blueberries
2 peaches, pitted and diced

1 To make the dough, mix the flour and salt in a bowl and rub in the butter with your fingertips until the mixture resembles breadcrumbs. Add 4 to 6 tablespoons cold water, 1 tablespoon at a time, and mix with a fork until it comes together to form a dough. Shape ⅔ of the dough into a ball and the remaining dough into a smaller ball, then wrap each ball in plastic wrap and chill in the refrigerator 30 minutes.

2 Dust a piece of parchment paper with flour. Take ⅔ of the dough and roll out into a circle about 12½ inches in diameter and trim around the edges, using a sharp knife, to neaten. Put a 10-inch pie plate, face-down, on top of the dough, then, holding the parchment paper and pie plate together, turn them over to drop the dough into the dish. Ease the dough into place, pressing down gently to remove any air pockets. Neaten the edge using a sharp knife.

3 To make the filling, put the flour, cornstarch, rice malt syrup, nutmeg, salt, lemon juice and lemon zest in a bowl and mix until combined.   Add the blueberries and peaches and mix well. Pour the filling into the dough-lined pie plate and level the surface with a spatula.

4 Preheat the oven to 450°F. Dust another piece of parchment paper with flour, take the remaining dough and roll out into a circle about 10¾ inches in diameter and trim around the edges, using a sharp knife, to neaten. Ease the dough onto the top of the pie and press down around the rim with your fingers to seal and crimp the edge. Using a sharp knife, cut a small cross in the center of the dough lid.

5 Bake 10 minutes, then turn the heat down to 350°F and bake 35 to 40 minutes longer until the crust is lightly browned and the juices are bubbling through the air hole. Remove from the oven and let cool in the pie plate 5 minutes. Serve warm or at room temperature.

 BAKED PEACH PUREE
Put 5 tablespoons of the peaches and 1 tablespoon water in a ramekin. Bake as above 15 minutes until the peaches are completely soft. Transfer to a blender and blend 30 seconds, adding water 1 teaspoon at a time, until smooth. Serve warm.

 BAKED PEACHES & BLUEBERRIES
Put 3 tablespoons each of the peaches and blueberries and 1 tablespoon water in ramekin. Bake as above 15 minutes until the fruit is completely soft. Transfer to a blender and pulse 15 seconds, adding water 1 teaspoon at a time, until the mixture forms a lumpy puree. Serve warm.

Here is a gorgeous tart. Bake it when plums and blackberries are at their peak in the summer. You can use other fruits, such as peaches, nectarines, cherries, strawberries or blueberries. I often let the children bake mini versions of this alongside the big one—just bake them for less time.

Plum & Blackberry Tart

SERVES: 10
PREPARATION TIME: 35 minutes, plus 30 minutes chilling
COOKING TIME: 40 minutes
STORAGE: Refrigerate up to 3 days.

....

FOR THE DOUGH
2 cups wholegrain spelt flour or wholewheat flour, plus extra for dusting
heaped ⅓ cup cane sugar
1½ teaspoons fine sea salt
½ cup (1 stick) plus 1 tablespoon chilled unsalted butter, diced

FOR THE FILLING
4 tablespoons wholegrain spelt flour or wholewheat flour
1 tablespoon cornstarch, ground arrowroot or kuzu
2 pounds plums, pitted and chopped
1 cup blackberries
⅓ cup rice malt syrup or heaped ¼ cup cane sugar
2 tablespoons lemon juice
plain yogurt, to serve

1 Grease a 12-inch shallow, fluted tart pan with oil. To make the dough, mix the flour, sugar and salt in a large mixing bowl and rub in the butter with your fingertips until the mixture resembles breadcrumbs. Add 2 to 3 tablespoons cold water, 1 tablespoon at a time, and mix with a fork until it comes together to form a dough. Shape the dough into a ball, wrap in plastic wrap and chill in the refrigerator 30 minutes.

2 Dust a piece of parchment paper with flour and roll out the dough into a circle about 14 inches in diameter and trim around the edges, using a sharp knife, to neaten. Put the pan, face-down, on top of the dough, then, holding the parchment paper and pan together, turn them over to drop the dough into the pan. Ease the dough into place, pressing down gently to remove any air pockets. Neaten the edge using a sharp knife.

3 Preheat the oven to 350°F. To make the filling, mix together the flour and cornstarch in a large bowl. Add the plums, blackberries, rice malt syrup and lemon juice and mix well. Spoon the mixture over the dough and smooth the surface with a spatula.

4 Bake 40 minutes until the top is bubbling. Remove from the oven and let cool 5 minutes, then turn out of the pan, transfer to a cooling rack and let cool. Serve warm or at room temperature with yogurt.

(6-9)

BAKED PLUM PUREE
Put 5 tablespoons of the plums and 1 tablespoon water in a ramekin and bake as above 15 minutes until completely soft. Transfer to a blender and blend 30 seconds, adding water 1 teaspoon at a time, until smooth. Serve warm.

(9-12)

BAKED PLUMS & BLACKBERRIES
Put 3 tablespoons each of the plums and blackberries and 1 tablespoon water in a ramekin and bake as above 15 minutes until completely soft. Transfer to a blender and pulse 15 seconds, adding water 1 teaspoon at a time, until the mixture forms a lumpy puree. Serve warm.

It's easier than you think pitting cherries, and this dessert is so delicious that it's worth the effort (just make sure you buy a cherry pitter to help you). If you don't have the time, however, you can use frozen or canned, unsweetened cherries instead.

Cherry Crumbles

MAKES: 4
PREPARATION TIME: 30 minutes
COOKING TIME: 30 minutes
STORAGE: Refrigerate up to 3 days.

....

FOR THE TOPPING
heaped ¼ cup cane sugar
½ cup wholegrain spelt flour or
   wholewheat flour
½ teaspoon fine sea salt
3 tablespoons sunflower oil, plus extra
   for greasing
plain yogurt, to serve

FOR THE FILLING
2 tablespoons cornstarch, ground
   arrowroot or kuzu
1 pound 2 ounces fresh, pitted cherries
   or frozen or canned pitted cherries
2 teaspoons lemon juice
1 teaspoon lemon zest
½ teaspoon vanilla extract

1 Preheat the oven to 375°F and grease four scant 1 cup to 1 cup ramekins or custard cups with oil. To make the filling, put the cornstarch and 3 tablespoons cold water in a bowl and mix together to make a smooth paste. **(6-9) (9-12)** Add the cherries, lemon juice, lemon zest and vanilla extract and stir until mixed well. Spoon the mixture evenly into the ramekins.

2 In another bowl, mix together the sugar, flour, salt and oil until just combined and the mixture resembles coarse breadcrumbs. Spoon the mixture evenly over the cherries. Bake 25 to 30 minutes until bubbling and lightly browned. Remove from the oven and let cool 5 minutes. Serve warm with yogurt.

(6-9) **CHERRY PUREE**
Put 5 tablespoons of the cherries and 2 tablespoons water in a blender. Blend 30 seconds, adding extra water 1 teaspoon at a time, until smooth. Serve warm or at room temperature.

(9-12) **BAKED CHERRIES WITH YOGURT**
Put 4 tablespoons of the cherries and 2 tablespoons water in a ramekin and bake as above 15 minutes until completely soft. Transfer to a blender and add 2 tablespoons of yogurt. Pulse 15 seconds, adding water 1 teaspoon at a time, until the mixture forms a lumpy puree. Serve warm.

One of my favorites. It's so good that it's hard to resist at any time of day and I find myself wanting it for breakfast. My girlfriend Jazz says her son Jonah always talks about the wonders of my crumble.

Rhubarb Raspberry Crumble

SERVES: 2 adults, 1 child and 1 baby
PREPARATION TIME: 20 minutes
COOKING TIME: 1 hour
STORAGE: Store in an airtight container up to 2 days, then refrigerate up to 3 days.

....

1 pound fresh or defrosted, frozen rhubarb, chopped
heaped 2½ cups fresh or defrosted, frozen raspberries
¾ cup plus 2 tablespoons cane sugar
plain yogurt, to serve

FOR THE CRUMBLE
heaped 1⅔ cups wholegrain spelt flour or wholewheat flour
¾ cup rolled oats
¼ cup buckwheat flakes
heaped ½ cup cane sugar
1½ teaspoons ground cinnamon
½ teaspoon fine sea salt
½ cup (1 stick) plus 1 tablespoon unsalted butter or sunflower oil, plus extra for greasing

1 Preheat the oven to 325°F and grease a 9 x 9-inch baking pan with butter. (6-9) (9-12) To make the crumble, put the flour, oats, buckwheat flakes, sugar, cinnamon and salt in a large mixing bowl and mix well. Heat the butter in a saucepan over low heat until melted, then remove from the heat. Add the melted butter to the flour mixture and stir until the mixture resembles coarse breadcrumbs. Spread ⅔ of the crumble mixture over the bottom of the baking pan, pressing down firmly with the back of a metal spoon. Leave the remaining crumble to one side.

2 In another bowl, mix together the rhubarb, raspberries and sugar. Pour the fruit mixture on top of the crumble mixture in the baking pan, then evenly sprinkle the remaining crumble mixture over the top. Bake 50 to 60 minutes until lightly browned. Serve warm or cold with yogurt.

(6-9) **OAT & BUCKWHEAT OATMEAL PUREE**
Put 2 tablespoons each of the oats and buckwheat flakes, 1 teaspoon of yogurt and ¾ cup water in a saucepan. Let soak, covered, 7 hours or overnight at room temperature. Bring to a simmer over high heat, then turn the heat down to low and cook, stirring occasionally, 10 minutes until completely soft. Transfer to a blender and add 2 tablespoons water. Blend 30 seconds, adding extra water 1 teaspoon at a time, until smooth. Serve warm.

(9-12) **OAT, BUCKWHEAT, RHUBARB & RASPBERRY OATMEAL**
Put 6 rhubarb pieces, 2 tablespoons each of the oats and buckwheat flakes, 1 teaspoon of yogurt and ¾ cup water in a saucepan. Let soak, covered, 7 hours or overnight at room temperature. Bring to a simmer over high heat, then turn the heat down to low and cook, stirring occasionally, 10 minutes until completely soft. Transfer to a blender and add 1 tablespoon of the raspberries and 2 tablespoons water. Pulse 15 seconds, adding extra water 1 teaspoon at a time, until the mixture forms a lumpy puree. Serve warm.

Sometimes it's nice to have the delight of a pie—without the bother of the pastry. My sister Jan says her kids prefer this version to hers, even though mine uses a lot less sugar.

Apple Dessert with Walnuts

SERVES: 8
PREPARATION TIME: 25 minutes
COOKING TIME: 1 hour
STORAGE: Store in an airtight container up to 2 days, then refrigerate up to 3 days.

....

FOR THE FILLING
3 tablespoons wholegrain spelt flour or wholewheat flour
heaped ¼ cup cane sugar
1 teaspoon ground cinnamon
¼ teaspoon ground nutmeg
½ teaspoon fine sea salt
1 pound 5 ounces sweet apples, cored and chopped
1 tablespoon lemon juice

FOR THE TOPPING
scant ½ cup wholegrain spelt flour or wholewheat flour
⅓ cup buckwheat flakes
¼ cup walnuts, coarsely chopped
1 ounce cane sugar
⅛ teaspoon fine sea salt
3 tablespoons chilled unsalted butter, diced, plus extra for greasing
plain yogurt, to serve

1 Preheat the oven to 350°F and grease a 10-inch pie plate with butter. To make the filling, put the flour, sugar, cinnamon, nutmeg and salt in a large mixing bowl and mix well. **(9-12)** Put the apples in a small bowl and sprinkle the lemon juice over them. Add to the flour mixture and mix well.

2 **(6-9)** To make the topping, put the flour, buckwheat flakes, walnuts, sugar and salt in a small bowl and mix well. Rub in the butter with your fingertips until the mixture resembles breadcrumbs. Put the apple mixture in the pie plate and spoon the topping mixture over the top. Bake 50 to 60 minutes until the filling is bubbling and the topping has browned. Serve hot with yogurt.

6-9 **BAKED BUCKWHEAT PUREE**
Put 4 tablespoons of the buckwheat flakes, 1 teaspoon of yogurt and ½ cup water in a small baking dish. Let soak, covered, 7 hours or overnight at room temperature. Bake as above 35 minutes until completely soft. Transfer to a blender and add 2 tablespoons water. Blend 30 seconds, adding extra water 1 teaspoon at a time, until smooth. Serve warm.

9-12 **BAKED BUTTERY APPLE & BUCKWHEAT**
Put 4 tablespoons of the buckwheat flakes, 1 teaspoon of yogurt and ½ cup water in a small baking dish. Let soak, covered, 7 hours or overnight at room temperature. Add 6 apple pieces and 1 teaspoon of the butter and mix well. Bake as above 35 minutes until the apple is completely soft. Transfer to a blender and add 2 tablespoons water. Pulse 15 seconds, adding extra water 1 teaspoon at a time, until the mixture forms a lumpy puree. Serve warm.

Loaded with fruit, this is a cross between a sheet cake and a pie. Brian and I have this for breakfast with a big blob of yogurt; Jessie and Nicholas take it to school for their snack; and little Cassie likes it anytime.

Apple & Blueberry Squares

SERVES: 2 adults, 1 child and 1 baby
PREPARATION TIME: 20 minutes
COOKING TIME: 50 minutes
STORAGE: Store in an airtight container up to 2 days, then refrigerate up to 3 days.

....

heaped 2 cups fresh or defrosted, frozen blueberries
10½ ounces apples, cored and chopped
1 tablespoon lemon juice
1 tablespoon cornstarch, ground arrowroot or kuzu
1½ cups rolled oats
½ cup buckwheat flakes
heaped ½ cup cane sugar
1 teaspoon baking powder
½ teaspoon fine sea salt
6 tablespoons sunflower oil, plus extra for greasing
1 teaspoon vanilla extract

1 Preheat the oven to 350°F and grease a 7½ x 10½-inch baking pan with oil. (6-9) (9-12) In a large bowl, mix the blueberries, apples, lemon juice and cornstarch and set aside. In another bowl, mix together the oats, buckwheat flakes, sugar, baking powder and salt. Add the oil, vanilla extract and scant ⅔ cup water and mix until well combined.

2 Spread the oat mixture in the bottom of the baking pan and smooth the surface with a spatula. Pour the blueberry mixture over the top and smooth the surface again. Bake 50 minutes until the top is bubbling. Remove from the oven and let cool 5 minutes. Cut into squares and serve warm or at room temperature.

(6-9) **BAKED APPLE & BUCKWHEAT PUREE**
Put 6 apple pieces, 4 tablespoons of the buckwheat flakes and ¾ cup water in a bowl and mix. Transfer to a greased ramekin and bake as above 35 minutes until completely soft. Transfer to a blender and add 2 tablespoons water. Blend 30 seconds, adding extra water 1 teaspoon at a time, until smooth. Serve warm.

(9-12) **BAKED APPLE & BLUEBERRY**
Put 1½ tablespoons each of the apples and blueberries, 4 tablespoons of the buckwheat flakes and 4 tablespoons water in a bowl and mix. Transfer to a greased ramekin and bake as above 35 minutes until completely soft. Transfer to a blender and add 2 tablespoons water. Pulse 15 seconds, adding extra water 1 teaspoon at a time, until the mixture forms a lumpy puree. Serve warm.

Who doesn't love rice pudding? It's a dish you can stick in the oven and let cook to perfection. Gently spiced and with sweet raisins, here is a healthy treat for everyone.

Oven Rice Pudding

SERVES: 2 adults, 1 child and 1 baby
PREPARATION TIME: 20 minutes, plus at least 7 hours soaking
COOKING TIME: 2 hours
STORAGE: Refrigerate up to 3 days.

....

heaped 1 cup sweet brown rice or
   short-grain brown rice
1 tablespoon plain yogurt
2 extra-large eggs
heaped ⅓ cup cane sugar
3 cups oat milk or rice milk
¼ cup raisins, chopped
1 teaspoon vanilla extract
1 teaspoon ground cinnamon
¼ teaspoon ground nutmeg
1 teaspoon fine sea salt

1 Put the rice and yogurt in a deep baking dish and cover generously with warm water. Leave to soak, covered, 7 hours or overnight at room temperature. **6-9** **9-12**

2 Preheat the oven to 325°F. Drain and rinse the rice, then return to the baking dish. In a small bowl, lightly beat the eggs together with a whisk. Add the eggs, sugar, oat milk, raisins, vanilla extract, cinnamon, nutmeg and salt to the baking dish and whisk until the sugar has dissolved and the cinnamon and nutmeg have dispersed.

3 Bake 30 minutes until a brown skin has formed on top of the pudding. Stir in the skin and bake 15 minutes longer. Stir again and bake 1 hour 15 minutes longer until the rice is completely soft and the top has browned. Serve hot or cold.

6-9 **SWEET RICE BAKE PUREE**
Put 2 tablespoons of the soaked rice and 8 tablespoons of the oat milk in a small baking dish and mix. Bake as above 1 hour 15 minutes until the rice is completely soft. Transfer to a blender and add 2 tablespoons water. Blend 30 seconds, adding extra water 1 teaspoon at a time, until smooth. Serve warm.

9-12 **SWEET RICE & RAISIN PUDDING**
Put 2 tablespoons of the soaked rice, 8 tablespoons of the oat milk and 1 teaspoon of the raisins in a small baking dish and mix. Bake as above 1 hour 15 minutes until the rice is completely soft. Transfer to a blender and add 2 tablespoons water. Pulse 15 seconds, adding extra water 1 teaspoon at a time, until the mixture forms a lumpy puree. Serve warm.

My husband Brian was dubious when I first created this, because it looks a little strange in the making. But once it was finished, I couldn't keep him away. It has a beautiful color and the flavors of a crisp fall and of Christmas.

Pumpkin Pudding

SERVES: 2 adults, 1 child and 1 baby
PREPARATION TIME: 20 minutes, plus cooling, plus at least 1 hour setting
COOKING TIME: 50 minutes
STORAGE: Refrigerate up to 3 days.

....

2 cups plain yogurt, plus extra to serve (optional)
heaped ½ cup cane sugar
1½ teaspoons ground cinnamon
½ teaspoon ground nutmeg
½ teaspoon ground cloves
½ teaspoon ground allspice
½ teaspoon fine sea salt
11¼ ounces pumpkin, peeled, seeded and diced or squash, seeded and diced
5½ tablespoons chilled unsalted butter, diced

1 Preheat the oven to 350°F. (9-12) In a bowl, mix together the yogurt, sugar, spices and salt. (6-9) Put the pumpkin, butter and spice mixture in a baking dish and mix, making sure the pumpkin is covered in the spice mixture.

2 Bake, covered, 50 minutes until soft. Remove from the oven and let cool completely. Transfer the mixture to a blender and blend 1 minute until smooth. Spoon the mixture into serving dishes. Cover with plastic wrap and let set in the refrigerator at least 1 hour. Serve cold with extra yogurt, if you like.

(6-9) BAKED PUMPKIN PUREE
Put 5 tablespoons of the pumpkin and 1 tablespoon water in a ramekin. Bake as above 30 minutes until the pumpkin is completely soft. Transfer to a blender and add 3 tablespoons water. Blend 30 seconds, adding extra water 1 teaspoon at a time, until smooth. Serve warm.

(9-12) BAKED PUMPKIN WITH YOGURT
Put 5 tablespoons of the pumpkin, 1 tablespoon water and 1 teaspoon of the butter in a ramekin. Bake as above 30 minutes until the pumpkin is completely soft. Transfer to a blender and add 2 tablespoons of the yogurt and 2 tablespoons water. Pulse 15 seconds, adding extra water 1 teaspoon at a time, until the mixture forms a lumpy puree. Serve warm.

I grew up on baked squash and love the smell of cinnamon and melting butter that wafts from the oven while it bakes. This version, with the apple and chopped pecans, is delightful.

Cinnamon Acorn Squash

SERVES: 2 adults, 1 child and 1 baby
PREPARATION TIME: 15 minutes
COOKING TIME: 50 minutes
STORAGE: Refrigerate up to 3 days.

....

extra virgin olive oil, for greasing
2 acorn squash, halved and seeded
2 apples, cored and chopped
heaped ¼ cup pecans, chopped
2 teaspoons rice malt syrup or
   1 teaspoon cane sugar
¼ teaspoon ground cinnamon
1 tablespoon unsalted butter

1 Preheat the oven to 350°F and grease a large baking dish with oil. Put the squash halves flesh-side down in the baking dish and bake 30 minutes until softening. Remove from the oven and turn the squash halves skin-side down in the baking dish.

2 Put the apples, pecans, rice malt syrup and cinnamon in a bowl and mix well. Spoon the apple mixture into each squash half until filled to the top. Divide the butter into 4 pieces and put 1 piece on top of each squash half. Bake 20 minutes until the squash and apples are soft. Serve hot.

(6-9) BAKED SQUASH & APPLE PUREE
Put ½ of 1 squash skin-side down in a greased baking dish and fill with 2 tablespoons of the apple. Bake as above 25 minutes until the squash and apple are completely soft. Transfer to a blender and blend 30 seconds, adding water 1 teaspoon at a time, until smooth. Serve warm.

(9-12) BAKED BUTTERY SQUASH & APPLE
Put ½ of 1 squash skin-side down in a greased baking dish and fill with 2 tablespoons of the apple and 1 teaspoon of the butter. Bake as above 25 minutes until the squash and apple are completely soft. Transfer to a blender and pulse 15 seconds, adding water 1 teaspoon at a time, until the mixture forms a lumpy puree. Serve warm.

An interesting marriage of fruit and root, this has a lovely sweetness. The combination of fruit and vegetable provides a great mix of nutrients as well, and it's a quick dish to prepare.

Banana & Sweet Potato Pudding

SERVES: 2 adults, 1 child and 1 baby
PREPARATION TIME: 20 minutes
COOKING TIME: 1 hour
STORAGE: Refrigerate up to 3 days.

....

unsalted butter, for greasing
8 ounces sweet potato, diced
2 cups wholegrain spelt flour or
    wholewheat flour
heaped ½ cup cane sugar
1 teaspoon ground cinnamon
¼ teaspoon ground nutmeg
½ teaspoon fine sea salt
1 extra-large egg
1¾ cup oat milk or rice milk
8 tablespoons sunflower oil
1½ teaspoons vanilla extract
2 bananas, quartered lengthwise
    and chopped
plain yogurt, to serve

1 Preheat the oven to 350°F and grease a baking dish with butter. Put the sweet potato in a steamer and steam, covered, 15 minutes until completely soft. Transfer to a bowl and mash thoroughly until smooth. (6-9) (9-12)

2 In a large mixing bowl, mix together the flour, sugar, cinnamon, nutmeg and salt. In another bowl, lightly beat the egg with a whisk, then add the oat milk, oil, vanilla extract, bananas and mashed sweet potato and mix. Add the egg mixture to the flour mixture and stir until combined. Pour the mixture into the baking dish and bake 45 minutes until lightly browned and set. Remove from the oven and let cool 5 minutes. Serve hot with yogurt.

(6-9) BAKED BANANA & SWEET POTATO PUREE
Put 6 banana pieces in a bowl and mash well. Add 3 tablespoons of the mashed sweet potato and 1 tablespoon water and mix well. Transfer to a greased ramekin and bake as above 20 minutes until lightly browned and set. Remove from the oven and let cool slightly. Transfer to a blender and add 1 tablespoon water. Blend 30 seconds, adding extra water 1 teaspoon at a time, until smooth. Serve warm.

(9-12) BAKED BANANA & SWEET POTATO
Put 6 banana pieces in a bowl and mash well. Add 3 tablespoons of the mashed sweet potato, 1 teaspoon of the oil and 1 tablespoon water and mix well. Transfer to a greased ramekin and bake as above 20 minutes until lightly browned and set. Remove from the oven and let cool slightly. Transfer to a blender and add 1 tablespoon water. Pulse 15 seconds, adding extra water 1 teaspoon at a time, until the mixture forms a lumpy puree. Serve warm.

Index